Däumel   Concrete in the Garden

Prof. Dr Gerd Däumel, Landscape Architect

Concrete in the Garden

Translated by C. van Amerongen, MSc, MICE

Elsevier Publishing Company Limited
London and Amsterdam
1971

ELSEVIER PUBLISHING COMPANY LTD
BARKING, ESSEX, ENGLAND

ELSEVIER PUBLISHING COMPANY
335 JAN VAN GALENSTRAAT, P.O. BOX 211, AMSTERDAM
THE NETHERLANDS

444-20068 1

LIBRARY OF CONGRESS CATALOG CARD NUMBER 76-122952

WITH 95 ILLUSTRATIONS

TRANSLATED FROM THE ORIGINAL GERMAN
BETON IM GARTEN BY C. VAN AMERONGEN

© 1963, 1968 BETON-VERLAG GmbH, DÜSSELDORF

© 1971 FOR THE ENGLISH TRANSLATION
ELSEVIER PUBLISHING COMPANY LIMITED

Printed in Great Britain by The Millbrook Press Limited, Southampton, England

Preface to the fourth edition

Concrete in the Garden is now in its fourth edition. Its predecessors were so favourably received by the readers that it has been possible to enrich this latest edition with many new illustrations and additional information on fair-faced concrete and exposed-aggregate concrete.

The basic conception remains unchanged. The purpose of this book is to point out the possibilities of concrete and cast stone in the garden and in landscape gardening and to encourage the use of this modern construction material. In addition, it gives hints on the use and methods of treating the material for different types of work.

Concrete has become very much a feature of present-day life and of architecture, which would hardly be conceivable without it. It is the construction material of our time. By utilizing its services in the garden we are being up to date and practical, and by availing ourselves of its numerous possibilities for shaping and surface finishes we can obtain aesthetically pleasing results. Concrete is a material that can enhance and enrich our enjoyment of gardens.

If this book succeeds in stimulating readers to make intelligent and correct use of concrete as a construction material in their gardens, without letting themselves be tempted into slavishly copying the examples presented, it will have excellently fulfilled its purpose.

Geisenheim, September 1968   *Gerd Däumel*

Contents

Introduction

Carefully made concrete with aggregrates selected for shape and colour, or concrete with a pleasingly textured surface, has achieved an accepted place for itself in the garden.

Concrete occupies an equivalent position with stone and brick in landscape gardening. It is essential, however, that concrete should be recognizable as a material in its own right, instead of misguidedly being disguised to look like something else. Any attempt to imitate the appearance of natural stone or other materials is to be deprecated. An example of extreme bad taste is afforded by those hideous garden seats and fences constructed of reinforced concrete got up to look like gnarled oak logs. Concrete which is expertly made and correctly used, with proper regard for its special characteristics, develops a distinctive beauty of its own.

Concrete is a mouldable material which, on setting, is transformed from a more or less plastic condition to a kind of stone. When this happens, the cement paste, consisting of cement and water, grows hard and thereby bonds the aggregate particles (gravel and sand) into an artificial conglomerate. Quite a number of natural rock materials of similar character are known, likewise consisting of conglomerations of heterogeneous constituents solidly bonded together. Of course, in conventional masonry the stones or bricks are also bonded into a solid structure with the aid of mortar. With concrete, however, the whole mass within the formwork (or shuttering) is turned into a monolith during the setting process, progressively acquiring better and better structural properties as it subsequently hardens.

In terms of appearance and strength concrete is in no way inferior to other materials used in landscape gardening, and a factor which more particularly favours its use is that it is economical. Difficulties of supply encountered with other materials often cause the landscape gardener to turn to concrete as his construction material. Another important reason for using concrete – precast concrete, in particular – is that it is often difficult to secure the services of properly skilled stone-masons. Correctly laying natural stone blocks or slabs with their varying thicknesses and sizes is not a thing that anyone can do. But landscape gardeners and indeed many laymen have no difficulty in dealing with concrete building blocks, which are of unvarying size, require no cutting or trimming, and seldom call for any after-treatment or subsequent dressing.

In the past, landscape gardeners were very reluctant to use concrete. This seems surprising, the more so as reinforced concrete construction originated with Joseph Monier [1823–1906] who was a professional gardener. He was the first to use iron reinforcement in concrete for making plant tubs, vases and bowls, some of which were used for decorating the

Vertical concrete planks set obliquely form a screen wall that gives privacy and yet allows air to circulate

Small enclosed garden with walls constructed of simple pierced precast concrete blocks

9

Even in the 'concrete garden' the plants are still the dominant features

roads and squares leading to the World Exhibition held in Paris in 1867. In the same year Monier was granted a patent for reinforced concrete, and this was followed by a further patent granted in 1871. Thus it was a gardener who established one of the most important principles of modern constructional science.

Concrete had indeed been widely used for a long time in horticulture for the construction of greenhouses, forcing frames, water supply basins and tanks, heating ducts and other installations. On the other hand, it was used only very sparingly in landscape gardening and was, even so, confined mainly to features installed on or in the ground. Around the turn of the century, however, concrete structures were making their appearance as ornamental features in gardens, more particularly in those designed by artists supporting the *art nouveau* movement. For example, a concrete pergola dating from that period is still in existence on the Mathildenhöhe at Darmstadt, Germany.

Even at later periods stone was still widely held to be the 'natural' material more suitable for use in gardens, while precast concrete was rejected as being merely an 'artificial' product – imitation stone. This school of thought considered that only 'natural' construction materials were permissible in gardens. Although the distinction between 'natural' and 'artificial' is purely a superficial one – for who would seriously assert that the constituents of concrete: gravel, sand and cement, are not in fact natural materials? – this view dies hard and even now still manifests itself. One deplorable consequence of this attitude was that precast concrete manufacturers tried to produce 'cast stone' or 'artificial stone' so cleverly composed as to be indistinguishable from natural stone. Yet precast concrete has no need for imitation, for it

Concrete paving slabs, footings and screen walls

Cast stone slabs separated by cobbled areas forming an interesting pattern

In-situ concrete paving enlivened by joints and different colouring of the individual bays *(see p.14)*

develops its own aesthetic qualities and, along with technical and economic advantages, it offers a considerable range of variety and adaptability. Limits upon its use are imposed only by considerations of economy in the manufacture of moulds and formwork.

There were two factors that ran counter to the adoption of concrete for general use in the more ambitious type of garden. For one thing, there was the monotonous colour of the material; secondly, its plain and uninterestingly featureless surface. Both these drawbacks have now been overcome. By using white cement and suitable colouring admixtures it is possible to obtain almost any shade of colour. Attractively textured surfaces of pleasing variety can be produced by the use of facing concrete, exposed selected aggregates and special surface treatments. So now there can no longer be any valid objections to the use of precast concrete in gardens. This has been demonstrated at all the German Federal Garden Shows, as well as those held in Vienna and Zürich, all affording

numerous examples of the excellent services that this material can render.

Houses, blocks of flats or public buildings of elegant modern design and constructed from up-to-date materials should not be incongruously tied up with gardens embodying such spurious 'romantic' features as shaky stepping stones and rustic work. The basic elements of the garden should be planned with clarity and precision, and the materials employed should be correspondingly clear and clean-cut. Elaborate artistic stonework in a garden is often something of an absurdity, since it is the plants, not stone, that should determine the character of the place. Stone in the form of walls, pavings or pergola columns is merely an aid to enable many different types of plants – shrubs, rose bushes, creepers, climbing plants, etc. – to be used to best advantage. A wall carefully constructed with considerable effort and expense, accurately finished joints and surfaces, and properly graded courses, often suffers the ultimate indignity of being concealed by plants. Hence in many cases — though by no means always — the cost of such a structure is hardly justified, and the use of a simpler material and less meticulous workmanship would be more appropriate.

It has long been known as a matter of experience that the basis for the usefulness and beauty of a garden is provided by carefully conceived design. No amount of lavish planting and care bestowed on the arrangement of the plants can cover up the defects of bad planning. It is therefore necessary, even when using so adaptable a material as concrete, to have clear-cut plans as to the subdivision of the garden, boundary demarcation, layouts of paths, size of terraces, arrangement of steps, location of ponds, pergolas, etc. People lacking extensive experience in the highly specialized field of garden planning would be well advised, even when contemplating changes in existing gardens, to consult a professional landscape gardener.

Whether one plans a strictly formal garden with straight flag-paved paths and rectangular flower beds and lawns, or an informal, irregular layout of the garden, or perhaps a judicious combination of the two, it will always be possible to establish a variety of designs whose constructional elements can advantageously be executed in concrete. This calls for imagination and ideas, but also for some measure of restraint. The garden should always be an 'outdoor room' which provides an agreeable open-air environment in which plants are the dominant feature determining its character. The purpose of the other materials is merely to make possible the use of plants and to serve, for example, as supports for plant tendrils, as lawn edgings or as stepping stones. This subservient function is of course common to all materials used in the garden.

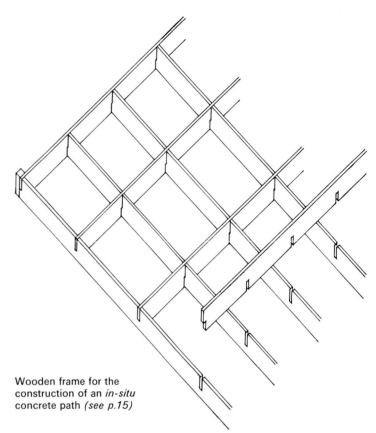

Wooden frame for the construction of an *in-situ* concrete path *(see p.15)*

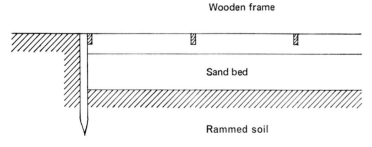

Constructing a path in *in-situ* concrete: cross-section *(see p.15)*

Possibilities for utilizing concrete in the garden are numerous, e.g., for foundations, walls, steps, pavings, pergolas, ponds and ornamental basins. It can also be used for a wide range of ornamental objects such as vases, bowls, plant tubs, fountains and bird baths of original design, sculpture, and all sorts of objects for children's play corners in gardens, terraces, boundary walls and interestingly shaped dividing walls within the garden itself can also be constructed in concrete. For the most commonly encountered features of gardens there exist ready-made (prefabricated) units — precast concrete — including more particularly slabs and building blocks which are of such quality and uniform size that even laymen can easily achieve good results with them.

Making one's own precast concrete units for garden use need present no difficulties if they are simple and not destined to carry structural loads. The essential thing is to use good concrete, i.e., concrete which is properly mixed and is made

Manhole rings filled with sand and provided with a water inlet make an ideal mud playground

with good aggregates and correctly proportioned constituents (cement, aggregates, water). With such concrete the gardener can carry out all his plans. He can add his own home-made concrete units to commercially purchased ones in order to adapt the latter to particular conditions and requirements. Since concrete units, once they have been installed, need no maintenance, the gardener can devote more time to his plants and their care.

In-situ concrete

There are two forms in which concrete may be used in gardens (as indeed in many other instances), namely, *in-situ* concrete and precast concrete. The term '*in situ*' is applied to concrete which is cast, in its final position, on the site of the construction job itself. The concrete, which must of course be placed in suitable formwork, may be mixed on the site, i.e., close to the point where it will actually be used, or it may alternatively be delivered to the site in a truck as ready-mixed concrete. 'Precast' refers to prefabricated concrete blocks, slabs or other units which are made in a factory or a casting yard and are installed on the job as ready-made, fully cured and hardened units. Each of these methods of using concrete has its own particular advantages and disadvantages.

In-situ concrete of suitably stiff consistency can often advantageously be used as a paving material for fairly large areas in gardens — e.g., terraces, seating areas, paths or roads. Such jointless paved areas are, however, inclined to be rather monotonous and lacking in character. In order to enliven the material and thus give it a more attractive appearance, as well as enabling it to undergo expansion movements, it is advisable to provide it with a suitable pattern of joints which are filled with bitumen or loamy sand. Such joints arranged in a pattern to subdivide a paved area are usually closer together than is technically necessary, but there is no objection to this if an aesthetically pleasing or interesting effect is achieved.

When concrete is placed *in situ*, it is necessary first to level the ground and to finish the adjacent soil to the correct levels to join up with the concrete. If additional earth has to be placed, it is very important to compact it carefully by ramming or, better still, with the help of a vibratory tamper. This compaction is essential in order to prevent any subsequent subsidence which might cause cracking or unsightly 'steps' in the concrete slab. When the soil under the future slab has been suitably compacted, the finished surface levels of the paving are established by means of stakes driven into the

Wall of a summer-house clad with concrete slabs studded with gravel

ground. The surface should always be constructed to a fall of between 0·5 per cent and 1 per cent, depending on the surface finish to be subsequently applied, in order to ensure proper run-off of water. This is particularly important in the case of large paved areas. Next, a layer of sand is spread uniformly on the compacted soil base and is then likewise compacted and watered. In the finished state the sand bed should be 7–10 cm ($2\frac{3}{4}$–4 in) thick and be so placed that its surface is 6–8 cm ($2\frac{1}{2}$–$3\frac{1}{4}$ in) below the surface level intended for the concrete slab. This last-mentioned dimension is therefore the thickness of the slab. Wooden frames, composed of boards or strips, for forming the desired pattern of joints are then laid on the sand bed, and the spaces between the boards (which thus serve as partitions) are filled with concrete. The concrete placed in each of these compartments should be compacted by tamping or ramming. With the aid of the wooden frames the concrete can be finished to the correct levels and any excess of concrete struck off. After the concrete has set, the boards or strips are removed, and the cavities left by them are filled with loamy sand, sifted earth or a bituminous compound. To enable the boards to be withdrawn easily and without damaging the edges of the concrete, it is advantageous to use boards which are of tapered cross-sectional shape (diminishing in thickness towards the bottom). Besides, the boards should be soaked with water before being placed on the sand bed, so that they will not undergo any further swelling due to absorption of water from the freshly placed concrete. If it is desired to construct fairly large slabs, it is advisable to provide them with mesh reinforcement. Welded fabric is very suitable for the purpose. Placing *in-situ* concrete in wooden frames in the manner described is an economical proposition only for extensive paved areas with a simple pattern of joints. For the construction of small slabs and complex shapes the cost is substantially greater.

Long narrow garden paths can, if *in-situ* concrete is to be used, advantageously be constructed with sliding formwork whose width is equal to that of the path. After the soil base for the path has been prepared in the manner already described for paved areas, the sliding form is placed at one end of the path and filled with freshly mixed concrete of relatively dry consistency. When the concrete has been tamped and smoothed, the partition is removed and the form is pulled forward a sufficient distance to enable the partition to be re-inserted. The position of the partition determines the thickness of the joints. The narrowest joint is formed when the partition is in direct contact with the previously laid

Paved terrace enlivened by varied pattern of joints and different surface finishes

section of concrete. Careful and prudent workmanship is necessary because the newly laid slab is very susceptible to damage for several hours.

Precast concrete

The principal advantages of precast concrete over *in-situ* concrete are that it is produced under conditions which enable better quality control and workmanship to be exercised than in the case of concrete made and used on the job. Besides, at a precasting works, concrete units which particularly require efficient curing can be treated with better care. However, in many cases the option of using either precast or *in-situ* concrete is not available and only one of the two alternatives is really practicable.

The term 'precast concrete' covers a wide variety of products

15

which can, broadly speaking, be classified into three groups: concrete products; concrete structural components; cast stone. The first of these groups, i.e., 'concrete products', is usually taken to comprise mass-produced (usually machine-made) articles of the precast concrete industry, e.g., solid or hollow building blocks, partition blocks, chimney blocks, roofing tiles and flooring slabs. They also include products which are more particularly of interest in the present context: concrete pipes, manhole and shaft units, cable ducts and, of course, the kerbs, paving slabs, paving setts, spur posts and boundary stones used in road construction. 'Structural components' are reinforced concrete or prestressed concrete units which may be complete in themselves, e.g., poles for overhead wires, fence posts, lighting columns, etc., or they may be assembled on the construction site to build larger structures, e.g., beams, columns, portal frames, roof slabs, floor slabs and wall panels. Finally, 'cast stone' (also known by such terms as 'artificial stone', 'reconstructed stone' or 'patent stone') comprises all those precast concrete products whose surfaces, in so far as the latter remain exposed and visible after the units have been installed, are given a special finish to improve their quality and appearance. Especially in parks and gardens the exposed concrete surfaces should not only be weather-resistant, structurally sound, indestructible and as inexpensive as possible, but should also be aesthetically pleasing. By the use of good cement, judicious choice of aggregates, suitable colouring and attractive surface treatment, cast stone units can be produced which constitute handsome and permanent features of our gardens.

Machine-made cast stone can be significantly cheaper than other comparable materials. Of course, the price will also depend to a great extent on the quantity and particular type of unit required. Special units which have to be purpose-made in limited quantities may hardly be cheaper than other materials. An important factor is that transport costs are generally low, since precast concrete works manufacturing cast stone products are to be found in nearly all the larger towns.

Another important argument in favour of using cast stone is that the stones are relatively light and can be installed by not-so-skilled labour. Craftsmen with special skills acquired as a result of long training and experience are not needed.

If the client and the landscape gardening consultant decide to use cast stone in a garden, it is of major importance to find stones that harmonize agreeably with the proposed buildings and other structural features. Nowadays more and more precast concrete manufacturers are offering paving slabs and building blocks – the most important components – in the same materials and with the same external finish. With steps the problem is more difficult. It is, of course, possible to use coloured slabs as treads and to provide these with a backing of

Garden seat formed by 'garden blocks', channel-shaped precast units

The same type of unit employed as a low retaining wall with pockets for plants

'Garden blocks' used to construct a smooth-faced retaining wall

A seat is formed by installing the units with the cavity facing forward

building blocks. To obtain monolithic steps in the same colour and finish as the paving slabs may be a harder problem to solve. Screen walls and ornamental walls, on the other hand, are usually such distinctive structural features that quite different blocks, often made with white cement, can appropriately be used for their construction.

Each type of precast concrete unit referred to above performs one particular function in the garden. Attempts have been made to develop construction elements which are versatile and can be employed for a wide variety of purposes in landscape gardening. An example of this was displayed at the Federal Garden Show at Stuttgart, where a square precast concrete unit with a channel-shaped cross-section was used both for a revetment wall and for a retaining wall. Depending on the positioning of the units, the top of the wall could be given a smooth continuous surface, in the manner of a coping, or alternatively, if the units were laid with their openings upwards, pockets were formed, through which the plants could be brought to the front of the wall. The same type of unit had also been utilized for the construction of various kinds of garden staircases, as well as a number of fixed garden seats. Furthermore, they had been used as bases for benches and raised platforms or had been assembled to form plant containers. A number of other applications could have been devised for these units, e.g., sand-boxes for children, play structures, flower bed edgings, staircase side walls, etc.

It is quite feasible to perform a wide range of functions and find satisfactory solutions for numerous problems with one simple construction element. The development of such versatile multi-purpose precast concrete units has been taken in hand by a number of manufacturers. Most useful would be a unit that could be employed both as a building block and as a paving slab.

A smaller variant of this garden unit is obtainable in southern Germany. It is the 'Lerag U' block, measuring 24 cm x 24 cm x 24 cm ($9\frac{1}{2}$ in x $9\frac{1}{2}$ in x $9\frac{1}{2}$ in) and weighing 19 kg (42 lb). Available in grey or red, it can be used for the construction of a variety of semi-open or closed walls in interesting patterns.

In Hesse a novel type of angle unit has been developed, which, in its shallow version, can be used as a kerbstone or for the construction of edgings to lawns. With the heavier version, retaining walls up to 50 cm (20 in) in height, seat walls, boundary walls or borders for raised flower beds can be built.

From southern Germany, more particularly the Stuttgart region, comes another versatile precast concrete unit which can be used for the construction of retaining walls, or as a facing material for walls, as well as for the construction of steps and edgings. Named 'Elementa', it is trough-shaped, 40 cm ($15\frac{3}{4}$ in) wide and 15 cm (6 in) deep, with standard lengths of 0·8 m (2 ft $7\frac{1}{2}$ in), 1·0 m (3 ft $3\frac{1}{2}$ in) and 1·2 m (3 ft $11\frac{1}{4}$ in). The unit has a wall thickness of 3·5 cm

Steps constructed with 'garden blocks' *(see p.16)*

Three units placed side by side form a bench. The wall behind the benches is constructed from units specially developed for garden walls

(1$\frac{3}{8}$ in). If desired, the external surfaces can be given a special finish, e.g., exposed aggregates. The advantage of the 'Elementa' units is that they combine large size with relatively low weight because of their hollow shape. By virtue of their special design (one of the longitudinal sides is formed with a slight batter) they can achieve interesting structural effects when used for retaining walls or for free-standing walls. Also, individual units may be made to protrude from the face of the wall and thus serve as seats, plant containers or other purposes.

With a little imagination and a fair knowledge of what is commercially available in this field, the landscape gardener may find interesting uses for precast concrete products that were originally intended for quite different purposes. Thus, square hollow blocks which are mass-produced for chimney construction can be used for building attractive partitions and ornamental walls. Thin concrete pipes can be assembled into useful columns for pergolas. The bottom part of a manhole or cesspit makes a splendid ornamental plant basin simply by recessing it into the ground. Coping slabs with an overhang of 5 cm (2 in) are laid on the edge. The basin is filled with water, and water-lilies are planted with roots nourished by soil in a basket at the bottom of the basin. The tapered top ring of the manhole when inverted, i.e., placed with the narrower opening downwards and filled with earth, makes an excellent plant tub at low cost.

To construct grassed areas which can carry a certain amount of vehicular traffic, various types of concrete turf blocks or slabs have been developed. In Germany the so-called 'B.G.' ('concrete + grass') slab, measuring 60 cm x 40 cm (23$\frac{1}{2}$ in x 15$\frac{3}{4}$ in) with an installed depth of 12 cm (4$\frac{3}{4}$ in), is most extensively used for the purpose. The 'slab' is actually a concrete grid comprising five 60 cm (23$\frac{1}{2}$ in) long strips interconnected by two transverse strips. This form of construction offers a number of technical and biological advantages. In gardens these units are used mainly on garage access drives and occasional parking areas. They are, however, also used for the paving of fire-engine roads around private or public multi-storey buildings. Other uses for these units are the construction of farm roads, grassed slope and bank revetments along watercourses, etc.*

The so-called 'Hartrasenplatte' ('hard turf slab') has been developed for similar purposes. This unit, measuring 40 cm x 60 cm (15$\frac{3}{4}$ in x 23$\frac{1}{2}$ in), is produced in thicknesses of 8 cm (3$\frac{1}{8}$ in) and 10 cm (4 in). In this type of turf unit the grass grows through four slot-like openings. In contrast with the previously mentioned slab, this one is reinforced and can carry loads of up to 12 tons. The units are not laid close up against one another; instead, gaps of 5 cm (2 in) width are left between them, in which grass also grows. This method of

*In Britain the 'B.G.' slab is manufactured by The Mono Concrete Co. Ltd., West Drayton, Middlesex.

Retaining wall constructed from coloured trapezoidal and triangular cast stone units

laying achieves a saving of 17 per cent in comparison with units placed in contact.

A larger variant of the well known 'SF' composite paving block is intended more particularly for the surfacing of grassed areas. The dimensions of this unit are 36 cm x 16 cm (14¼ in x 6¼ in), the thickness being 10 cm (4 in); it is pierced by two openings which are filled with earth in which grass grows. With all turf blocks or slabs, of whatever type, it is very important to ensure that the level of the earth in which the grass is rooted is 2–3 cm (about 1 in) below the top surface of the block or slab. Failure to observe this rule will result in the destruction of the lawn by the motor traffic.

Colouring of concrete

In recent years new colours and shapes, characteristic surface textures, and the use of exposed aggregate, have given added interest to cast stone products and have opened up wide scope for their use in gardens and parks. Further possibilities undoubtedly exist and are worth investigating. Once again, however, resistance has to be overcome – this time from the 'purists' who hold the view that the only right and genuine concrete is concrete whose surface texture has been produced by the direct imprint of the mould or formwork. Such people especially condemn exposure of the aggregate particles as falsification. There may indeed be technical structures for which it is important to retain the cement skin on the surface of the concrete; but with garden structures this is seldom the case. By exposing the aggregates and bringing out the texture of the concrete the true nature of this material as a con-glomerate is fully revealed.

Colouring the exposed surfaces and the use of white cement have hitherto been the most important techniques for embellishing the surface of concrete. The rather unattractive grey colour of concrete slabs was probably the deciding argument against their use in gardens. Coloured slabs or blocks give the material greater appeal and provide a good background for plants, which should always be the principal 'building material' in a garden.

In order to avoid the monotonous grey of large surfaces, these may be subdivided into smaller areas which are given different colours. Coloured concrete may be used in alternation with uncoloured concrete, or two differently coloured concrete mixes may be employed, or indeed two different shades of the same colour. First, all the slabs of one colour should be cast and then, as a second stage of the concreting operations, the slabs of the other colour. When using colouring media, it is necessary to proceed with caution; excessively conspicuous and bright colours are objectionable in a garden because they are distracting and thus tend to spoil the effect of the colours of the flowers.

Pigments used for the colouring of concrete should conform to a number of requirements. They should be compatible with cement, i.e., they must not attack the cement or be attacked by it. The pigments should not fade on prolonged exposure to sunshine. Also, they must not contain any substances that adversely affect the hardening process of the concrete. For red, yellow, brown and black colours the appropriate iron oxide pigments are employed. Titanium oxide is used for white. Manganese blue, which is non-fading and compatible with cement, is a suitable blue pigment. Green is obtained by using chromium oxide or chromium hydroxide. These are synthetic pigments produced from metals and metallic salts. Their purity and homogeneity make them very suitable as colouring materials for concrete. The quantity of pigment added to the concrete mix should preferably not exceed 5 per cent (by weight) of the cement. It is necessary to warn against a number of otherwise widely used pigments. Thus, the following are not suitable: red lead and cadmium red, chrome yellow and zinc yellow, lead white and zinc white, Paris, Berlin and Prussian blue, chrome green, carbon black and lamp black. With some pigments the strength of the concrete is not significantly impaired even if more than 5 per cent (by weight) is added to the mix. This is more particularly the case

Garden wall and horseshoe-shaped bench in fair-faced concrete *(see p.22)*

Fair-faced concrete wall with water outlets

Garden wall with interesting vertical pattern produced by the formwork

with manganese blue. In order to obtain as uniform a mixture of cement and pigment as possible, these two constituents should be mixed dry until a uniform shade of colour is obtained. Uniformity will certainly be achieved when the cement and the pigment are mixed in advance by mechanical means (mixing drum). Adequate uniformity can, however, also be obtained without such dry pre-mixing of the cement and pigment, if all the mix constituents are mixed in a pan-type concrete mixer until visual inspection shows the mix to have a uniform colour. This requires a longer mixing time than is normally employed for concrete.

In general, it is preferable to use subdued colours and colours moderated with grey. In recent years, however, slabs and blocks made with white cement and having bright colours

have also appeared on the market. This introduction of vivid colouring into cast stone products for garden use is strongly to be deprecated. A path constructed of gaudy red concrete flags will not only distract attention from even the finest roses, but is also liable to upset the spirit of tranquillity of the garden as a whole.

Of course, there are exceptional circumstances where strong concrete colours are permissible or indeed essential — for example, to subdivide and enliven large paved areas.

Excellent effects can be achieved with white constructional components, provided that the gardener takes care not to place white flowering plants in their immediate vicinity. Delicate pastel shades can be obtained by the addition of very small quantities of colouring media to white cement.

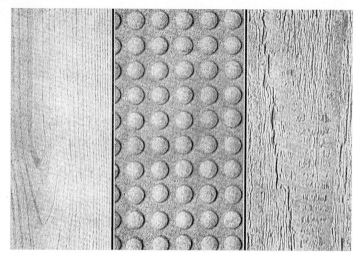

Fair-faced concrete patterns produced by wrought formwork boards, plastic formwork linings, and unwrought formwork boards

Fair-faced concrete

This term is applied to concrete surfaces which are intentionally left exposed to view as an architectural or aesthetic feature of a building or other structure and which are given an appropriate surface finish. A synonymous term is 'architectural concrete'. Sometimes the concept is restricted more particularly to concrete which has an 'off-the-form' texture, i.e., shows the imprint of the formwork, e.g., a board-marked pattern or a pattern produced by a special lining applied to the inner faces of the formwork.

Fair-faced concrete should have uniform surfaces which are as free from pores and 'blowholes' as possible. Also, the exposed surfaces of a structure should all be of the same shade of colour. Good dimensional accuracy and well finished edges or arrises free from blemishes are other requirements. The construction joints should be judiciously positioned and be kept inconspicuous.

Not only the shape but also the surface features of the concrete are determined by the mould or formwork against which it hardens. The planning and design of a structure should therefore include careful consideration of the choice of materials and of the design and construction of the formwork. In this context it should be borne in mind that not only the desired effects, such as, for example, the vertical pattern produced on the surface of a garden wall, but also the blemishes and the effects of poor workmanship in making the formwork, will show up on the finished structure.

Clearly, smooth surfaces of substantial size are more difficult to produce satisfactorily than textured or patterned ones. On smooth unbroken surfaces even the slightest irregularities or blemishes such as are liable to arise at the joints between the formwork panels, or in consequence of variations in the mix composition or the compaction of the concrete, will manifest themselves as defects. For this reason continuous smooth surfaces should not exceed about one square metre (10 ft²) in area. Large surfaces, such as those of a long garden wall, for instance, should either be suitably subdivided – which can be done by fixing strips of material having an appropriate cross-sectional shape to the formwork – or the surfaces should be given a distinctive rough texture of their own, e.g., by casting them against textured formwork.

As a result of subdividing large surfaces, independent areas are obtained which possess their own possibilities of aesthetic expression, convey an appropriate sense of scale, and make it easier for the viewer to survey and appreciate the garden as a whole. An important point is that such subdivision provides an effective means of masking or mitigating unintentional differences in colour, since each bay or panel functions to some extent as an independent unit. With rough-textured formwork the individual bays should not exceed about four square

Garden terrace paved with exposed-aggregate slabs. Added interest is obtained by the use of strips of paving of varying width

metres (40 ft²). In a large structure construction joints, i.e., joints in those positions where concreting is temporarily stopped for such a length of time that the concrete already placed sets before concreting is resumed, can hardly be avoided, since it is generally not possible to cast the concrete in one uninterrupted operation. The construction joints should be arranged to coincide with joints and boundaries between geometrical features of the structure and thus be kept as inconspicuous as possible.

Coarse-textured exposed concrete surfaces are obtained usually by means of formwork constructed from unwrought boards. The natural grain of the wood and the saw cuts produce a comparatively fine surface texture. To enhance this effect, the boards may be roughened by sandblasting. More strongly marked textures and patterns can be obtained with formwork consisting of boards varying in width and thickness or constructed from weatherboarding.

Other methods of enlivening the concrete surface consist in chamfering the edges of the boards or fixing strips of wood or other material on the inside of the formwork. Stronger contrasts are obtained by simultaneously using wrought and unwrought boards, laid in alternate directions. The horizontal or the vertical features of a structure can be accentuated by the use of appropriate profiling of the formwork. Relief effects can be obtained by the application of patterned linings to the formwork. Free ornamental shapes cut from wood or foam plastic can be attached to the inside of the formwork to produce sculptured concrete surfaces. For a limited number of uses (up to about 30 or 40) for small production series, rubber mats may be used as formwork lining if they have the desired pattern.

When horizontal strips are fixed to the inside of the formwork, it should be ensured that the concrete always properly fills it. To prevent damage to the arrises when the formwork is removed, the wooden strips should have a trapezoidal cross-sectional shape, with the larger base fixed to the formwork, so that they can easily be withdrawn from the concrete. With closely spaced ribs or similar raised features on the inner face of the formwork which produce a grooved pattern, the maximum particle size of the aggregate in the mix should be carefully controlled. Otherwise it may easily occur that coarse particles get jammed between the ribs and thus prevent the concrete from properly filling the interstices.

Vertical corners should be treated with particular care. To ensure that no unsightly gaps or gravel pockets are formed at

In-situ concrete wall in a garden. A modern sculptured effect has been obtained by means of shaped blocks attached to the inner face of the formwork, in conjunction with exposed-aggregate and sandblasted surface finishes

arrises despite careful compaction, it is advisable to chamfer the corners by fixing strips of triangular section in the corners of the formwork. This precaution will also make it easier for the concrete to fill the corners. Obviously, formwork should be properly braced by means of a strong supporting timber structure.

Exposed aggregate concrete

Besides surface finishes obtained direct from the formwork (or the patterned or textured lining placed in it), there are various surface finishes which are produced by subsequent mechanical or chemical treatment of the concrete after removal of the formwork. One of the best known techniques is that of exposing the aggregate particles.

The term 'exposed aggregate concrete' refers more particularly to surfaces in which the particles of gravel or other coarse aggregate have been exposed to view by scrubbing off the outer skin of cement before it has fully hardened. This technique can be used both for *in-situ* and for precast concrete. In the latter case, particularly when the concrete is made under factory conditions, various advantages due to closer quality control and the possibility of using power-operated mechanical equipment giving better results are available.

The exposed aggregate may be of a particular colour, or the desired aesthetic effect may be produced by using aggregates with special gradings or with particles of special shape. Furthermore, the cement may be coloured or may be made to contrast pleasingly with the colour of the aggregate.

Exposed aggregate concrete has come to be widely used in gardens and parks because experience with coloured concrete slabs has not always been very favourable. Either the colours were too harsh and 'drowned' the colours of the flowers or they faded or deteriorated under the action of sunlight and weather conditions. On the other hand, exposed aggregate concrete permanently retains the unvarying colour and fresh gleam of the aggregate particles (gravel or crushed stone chippings). If the rules of correct workmanship are applied, exposed aggregate concrete is very durable. If precasting works it is moreover possible to use facing concrete, i.e., a relatively thin layer of decorative concrete containing the desired special aggregate particles and applied over a backing layer of ordinary concrete.

For making exposed aggregate concrete, careful and conscientious workmanship is essential, as it is hardly possible to correct mistakes or repair damage. The aggregates employed should be accurately graded and the cement accurately batched. The colour, size and uniform distribution of the aggregate particles determine the appearance of the concrete surface. To obtain a favourable particle mixture, it is absolutely

necessary to add the aggregates in separate weighed quantities, each comprising a narrow particle size range. Gap gradings in which the medium-sized particles are absent have proved favourable for the purpose.

To be recommended are aggregate particle mixtures with 25 per cent of the particles in the 0–3 mm ($0-\frac{1}{8}$ in) range and 75 per cent in the 7–15 mm (approx. $\frac{1}{4}-\frac{5}{8}$ in) or the 15–30 mm (approx. $\frac{5}{8}-1\frac{1}{4}$ in) range. Instead of 15–30 mm gravel, stone chippings of 12–25 mm ($\frac{1}{2}-1$ in) size are sometimes used. If the concrete is densely reinforced, it is preferable to use a smaller maximum particle size, as this makes for better workability of the mix. Scrubbing or brushing the concrete to expose the aggregate particles is usually performed with power-driven mechanical equipment in precasting works; in the case of *in-situ* concrete, on the other hand, it generally has to be done with wire brushes or root fibre brushes. It is important not to remove too much cement mortar from the surface, or else the aggregate particles will drop out. They should still be firmly embedded on completion of the scrubbing operation. As a general rule, not more than about one-third of the particle surface should be exposed. Loosened particles which are not removed at the outset will become detached from the surface by frost action in winter. After the concrete has been brushed and the aggregate thus exposed, the surface must be washed down with clean water to remove the fine film of cement from the individual particles.

It is not possible to lay down a general rule as to how many hours after concreting should elapse before brushing is carried out. The length of time depends on the rate of setting of the concrete. If the material has already become too hard, brushing to expose the aggregate will be difficult or even impossible. On the other hand, if the formwork stripping and the brushing operations are done too early, the treatment may result in excessive removal of mortar, so that the surface texture of the concrete is loosened and the stability of the structure endangered. It may be necessary to carry out a test on the site, using the same materials, in order to determine empirically the correct length of time to wait between placing the concrete in the formwork and brushing the concrete surface to expose the aggregate. Factors affecting this length of time are weather conditions (temperature and humidity), the type of cement and its strength class, and the temperature of the freshly mixed concrete. In addition, it should be considered whether the available labour force on the job is sufficient to cope with the operations of stripping the formwork and brushing the concrete surface before nightfall or before the concrete

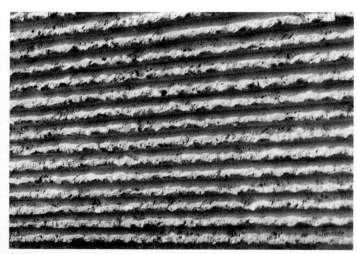

Ribbed concrete surfaces. After hardening, the ridges were broken by hammering to produce the desired effect

Slabs in modern shapes can achieve striking effects and serve to enliven large paved areas *(see p.29)*

becomes too hard. The final cleaning of the surface to remove the cement film may be done with dilute hydrochloric acid, but this treatment should always be followed by energetic washing down with clean water.

There exist a number of chemical agents which can retard or even prevent the setting of the cement at the surface of concrete. These setting retarders are applied uniformly to the inside of the formwork. Considerable care should be exercised in tamping or vibrating the concrete if such agents are used, so that they will not mix with the concrete. An alternative method, which obviates this risk, is to use paper which has been impregnated with a retarder and is glued to the inner surface of the formwork. The advantage of using a setting retarder is that it substantially increases the length of time available for carrying out the surface treatment and greatly facilitates it.

Concrete whose aggregate is to be exposed should be mixed with considerable care. When it is placed in the formwork, it should not be allowed to pour along the surfaces treated with a retarder. To prevent segregation, the mix should not be poured from any great height. In the construction of walls the concrete should be deposited in layers ('lifts') 30–50 cm (12–20 in) in depth.

Compaction can most advantageously be performed by means of high-frequency vibrators. Internal vibrators (or poker vibrators) should be quickly immersed and slowly withdrawn from the concrete. The compacting action should give the concrete a plastic consistency, but not turn it into a liquid. The vibrator should be inserted at points situated close enough together for the successive ranges of action to overlap.

Other surface treatments

Besides exposure of the aggregate particles by scrubbing (brushing), there are various mechanical methods of surface treatment for obtaining desired patterns or textures. Attractive surface finishes can be produced even by skilled use of the finishing float. A wooden float produces a less smooth surface than a steel trowel does. Rougher textures are obtained with a felt-covered float. Striated surfaces can be formed by brushing the young concrete with a stiff broom. With particular manipulations and rotational movements of the float it is possible to produce fan-shaped, shell-like or striped patterns, according to the skill and dexterity of the manipulator.

Parallel lines or V-shaped grooves can easily be formed, but are hardly attractive. A roller with raised features on its surface can be used to produce a pattern of small pits in the concrete. The roller should be handled with great care, because bad starts, deviations from straight lines and the crossing of lines create a very messy appearance.

Various treatments for exposing the texture of the concrete can be applied after it has hardened. These usually take the form of tooled finishes (point tooling, bush-hammering, granulating, etc.). Different degrees of contrast can be obtained by varying the intensity of the blows or strokes. Interesting finishes are also obtainable by sandblasting or grinding.

Foundations

One of the types of work that the landscape gardener has traditionally executed in concrete is the construction of footings or foundations for walls, staircases and other garden structures. Foundations are buried in the ground and serve to transmit the weight of the structure uniformly to the subsoil. As a safeguard against frost attack, foundations should always be installed below frost penetration depth, i.e., the bearing surface of the foundation on the subsoil should be from 0·80 m to 1·20 m (approx. 2 ft 6 in to 4 ft) below ground level, depending on regional climatic conditions. In the case of retaining walls which have to resist lateral earth pressure, and for high walls generally, the foundations should extend down to a loadbearing stratum. Soils possessing suitable bearing capacity are gravel, firm loam and clay soils, and rock. Humus, peat, mud and running sand are generally deficient in structural bearing capacity.

If loadbearing strata are located at considerable depth, so that construction of a complete foundation at that depth would be uneconomical, it is advisable to construct piers with individual footings extending down to those strata. These piers are surmounted by reinforced concrete capping beams which in turn form the base for carrying the wall or other structure.

The concrete used for foundation work should be of 'dry' consistency. It is laid in layers 15–20 cm (6–8 in) thick in the formwork or trench and is tamped until moisture begins to glisten faintly at the surface of each layer. The last layer, which must directly support the masonry, should be tamped and then struck off with a screeding beam which is moved along the top of two battens fixed at the correct level.

It is advisable to construct each structural member in a continuous operation, if possible. However, if construction joints are unavoidable, the 'old' concrete, i.e., the concrete which has already hardened, should be carefully cleaned, roughened and finally – a short time before concreting is resumed – coated with cement mortar to ensure good bond. Construction joints in foundations should always be located at sections which are structurally of minor importance, never at corners or at points which will subsequently be severely stressed. In order to obtain the largest possible contact surfaces between 'old' and 'new' concrete, the face of the construction joint should be sloped or, better still, stepped. If the 'old' concrete at the joint

Circular stepping stones and flat steps in combination with loose pebbles

Variety introduced into a paved area by the use of exposed-aggregate slabs

Hexagonal paving slabs, laid dry on a bed of sand. The fountain is of white concrete

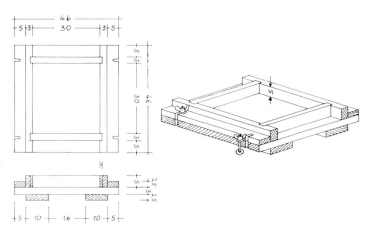

Wooden mould for making footpath slabs *(see p.33)*

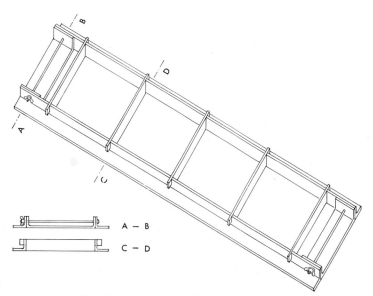

Mould made of angle-iron for casting four footpath slabs simultaneously

Steel mould for casting footpath slabs

After the concrete has been tamped, the corner connection is released and the mould removed from the slab

The empty mould is now reassembled for the casting of the next slab

has not yet hardened, it should be roughened with the edge of a trowel before fresh concrete is placed against it. At corners and edges the concrete should always be very carefully compacted.

Slab paving

Precast concrete or cast stone paving slabs, or 'flags' as they are often called, are widely used for the construction of paths and other paved areas in gardens and parks. They are commercially available in such a variety of shapes, colours and surface textures that the correct type of paving unit for any particular purpose can readily be found. Besides the usual square and rectangular slabs there are various other shapes which have been developed for specific purposes and duties or are based on aesthetic conceptions.

The landscape gardener will always strive to give emphasis to the unity of house and garden by using in the garden the same materials as those which have been used in the construction of the house. It would be contradictory and in deplorable taste if a modern building of reinforced concrete and glass were closely adjacent to a garden or park laid out with crazy-paving and 'rustic' features or 'romantic' rock-gardens.

One significant advantage of cast stone over natural stone has already been pointed out: the man-made product is dimensionally accurate, unvarying in size and thickness. This greatly facilitates the work of laying the slabs, which seldom require any additional cutting or trimming. The perfectly flat upper surface of the cast stone slabs makes them easy and comfortable to walk on. Besides, garden furniture can stand firmly and conveniently on terraces paved with cast stone slabs.

Manufacturers can fulfil nearly every requirement as to shape, colour and durability of their products. For the sake of economic production, however, they must concentrate on a limited number of practical slab sizes and conform to some degree of dimensional standardization. Because of mechanized manufacture, there is bound to be a certain amount of monotony in the material produced. Relatively large areas can nevertheless be pleasingly enlivened by using slabs of different colours in successive zones or by arranging them in appropriate patterns and/or using variously shaped slabs. On the other hand, smaller areas and paths should be paved with slabs all of the same type and colour or only varying slightly in colour.

Cast stone slabs as paving, garden seats and steps

Good ornamental effects and patterns can also be achieved with cast stone slabs with different surface finishes. For example, slabs with a smooth coloured surface may be alternated with exposed-aggregate slabs. In this way large paved areas can be enlivened in a very striking and attractive manner. On smaller areas a checkerboard pattern of two types of slab can suitably be employed. At the same time, it should be ensured that the slabs do not present a slippery surface. Adequate roughness to produce a safe walking surface can be obtained by the use of suitable aggregates, by exposing the aggregate particles, or by the use of special mould linings to produce the desired non-slip surface texture.

When slabs are to be laid in the open, some technical details call for attention. On arrival at the site, the slabs are offloaded from the vehicle and stacked. Each size of slab should be stacked separately. Exposed-aggregate slabs should be separated according to the colour of the aggregates and stored in the upright position.

If it is intended to lay the slabs on firm natural ground, an approximately 5 cm (2 in) thick sand bed, which should be

White fair-faced concrete footbridge over a curved pond with *in-situ* concrete edging

well compacted and levelled, will provide a suitable base. A layer of cement mortar, about 3 cm (1¼ in) thick and of plastic consistency, should be laid on this sand bed. Some lime may be added to the mortar. Next, the precast concrete slabs are laid on the mortar in accordance with the desired pattern. They are driven flush by laying a board over them and tapping it with a wooden mallet until the mortar is forced up into the joints to a height of about half the slab thickness. In carrying out this operation, care should be taken to ensure that the surfaces of the slabs do not become contaminated with mortar. The slabs should not be walked on for at least 24 hours.

If slabs are laid on fill material ('made ground'), as is often the case with house terraces and garden paths, the soil should be well compacted. Then a base course consisting of relatively low-strength concrete about 8–10 cm (3–4 in) thick should be placed on the compacted soil. This concrete may be provided with mesh reinforcement. When the base concrete has set, it is covered with 1·5–2 cm ($\frac{3}{4}$–$\frac{7}{8}$ in) thick layer of mortar, of similar composition to the one referred to in the preceding paragraph, and the slabs are then laid on the mortar and tapped flush.

Sometimes slabs are laid initially on fill material without the interposition of concrete and mortar. In that case the soil should be very thoroughly compacted and covered with a bed of sand. The slabs are laid directly on the sand, and sand should be carefully packed under them at the edges of the paving. Depending on the depth and degree of compaction of the fill, unequal settlement of the slabs is liable to occur. After a few years, when the ground has had time to consolidate, the slabs can be taken up, the ground levelled, and the slabs relaid on a mortar bed.

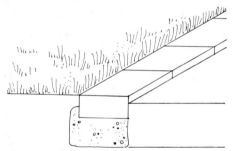

Raised kerb

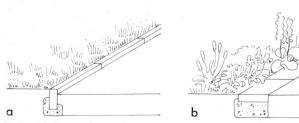
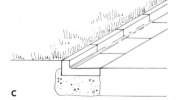
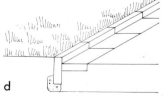

Various kerb structures: (a) simple kerb; (b) flat kerb; (c) Danish L-shaped kerb with channel; (d) kerb in combination with horizontal edge slabs forming a channel *(see p.34)*

The joints between precast concrete paving slabs should generally be 0·5 cm ($\frac{3}{16}$ in) wide. When the slabs have been laid the joints should be filled with sand mixed with some cohesive soil. This mixture should be brushed into the joints. On the other hand, if the joints are to be pointed, they should be made 1 cm ($\frac{3}{8}$ in) wide. For good workmanship, using a pointing tool, the joints should be filled either with a ready-to-use commercially available compound or with mortar consisting of one part of cement to two parts of sand. Care should be taken not to contaminate the surfaces of the slabs. Pointing does, it is true, add to the cost of the job, but offers some advantages : the joints are properly sealed, so that rainwater cannot wash out the filling, no weeds can grow in them, and the carefully planned pattern of the slabs and joints stands out more clearly.

The completed paving must not immediately be washed down with water, as this would cause the mortar to be washed out of the joints and adhere to the surfaces of the slabs. After drying, it would leave them covered with a grey coating which is difficult to remove. The mortar should therefore be given time to harden before water is applied.

Since the surface of an exposed-aggregate slab consists largely of gravel particles, which are exceedingly hard, such slabs cannot be cut by means of ordinary hand tools on the job. Any special-sized slabs required for forming the desired pattern

Ornamental screen wall constructed of hand-moulded units *(see p.43)*

Garden wall constructed of cast stone blocks. The coping is also of cast stone

Ornamental garden wall constructed of special shaped blocks

Garden wall constructed of blocks

Honeycomb units forming a screen wall

Concrete planks set obliquely provide protection for this seating area *(see p.44)*

must therefore be manufactured separately. Sometimes it is more convenient to use *in-situ* concrete, with an exposed aggregate finish, in places where precast purpose-made units would be difficult or expensive to manufacture, e.g., at curves in paths or around circular ponds. A simpler, but certainly not a better, solution consists in filling the awkward curved areas with cobble-stones. Sometimes slabs whose lateral faces have an inward slope (or batter) are used. Such slabs can, if so desired, be placed with their edges touching one another. The sloped sides ensure that the joints are open at the top.

A large proportion of commercially sold paving slabs are machine-made. Nevertheless, for garden use, slabs cast in open moulds can be advantageous, more particularly because they can be produced in a variety of shapes and offer more possibilities in surface treatment. Square or rectangular slabs are simplest to make, however. The surfaces can be smoothed, roughened or covered with embedded gravel particles. Special

units such as corners, slabs pierced with holes for plants or to serve as gulley gratings, etc. are easy to produce.

For garden purposes slab sizes ranging from 30 cm x 30 cm (about 1 ft x 1 ft) up to 60 cm x 60 cm (about 2 ft x 2 ft) are suitable. Larger slabs are too heavy, so that laying them becomes a difficult operation. On the other hand, slabs which are to be used as individual stepping stones, should not be too light, so as not to move when stepped on.

Wooden or steel moulds are used in making precast concrete paving slabs. If only a limited number of slabs have to be produced, a wooden mould will usually suffice. But if frequent re-use of the mould is envisaged, steel is the material to use, a good size being a 60 cm (2 ft) square mould made from angle-irons. The latter are welded together at two opposite corners in such a manner that one leg of the angle section forms a horizontal base, while the vertical other leg forms the side of the mould. At their free ends the angle-irons are pro-

A look through the dividing wall into the 'concrete garden'

paved surface, and give the edges some protection against being trodden off by pedestrians. These kerbs should not, however, protrude more than 5 cm (2 in) above the level of the paved surface, and the top of the kerb should be flush with the lawn.

Straight and curved kerb units (the latter in a range of radii) have long been commercially available. A later development has been the kerb of L-shaped cross-section, one leg of which serves to retain the edge of the lawn or planted area, while the other, laid flush with the paved surface, forms a rainwater channel. In cases where chemical weedkillers are used to keep gravel or waterbound macadam paved surfaces free from

Dividing wall of precast concrete units

vided with eyes which register over each other when the two L-shaped halves of the mould are assembled. The mould can then be locked by the insertion of a pin into each pair of eyes. When the mould has been filled, the concrete carefully tamped, and the surface treatment (if any) applied, the pins are withdrawn and the two halves removed. They can then be locked together again by means of the eyes and pins and be used for forming the next slab. By blocking out parts of the mould with strips of wood equal in thickness to the depth of the mould, it is possible to make any desired smaller size of slab.

It is necessary to warn against the use of concrete paving slabs of irregular or 'free-shaped' outline in the garden. Such attempts to imitate the irregular outlines of natural crazy-paving stones are to be deprecated.

Coping slabs on walls and similar structures are among the earliest products of the precast concrete industry. For many years they have been made in the traditional saddle shape, with drip throatings under the projecting edges.

On paths which are not paved with precast concrete slabs, but are instead provided with waterbound macadam surfacings, it is essential to install kerbs. These form a clear demarcation between the pathway or roadway and adjacent lawns or planted areas, prevent grass and weeds spreading on to the

Concrete wall with prominent relief-type features

Retaining wall constructed of cast stone blocks with pockets for plants

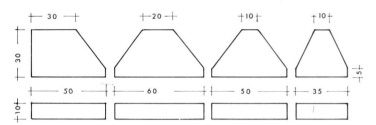

weeds it is necessary to use kerbs which rise higher above these surfaces. Weedkiller applied in spring remains on the surface for a long time. During heavy showers the splashing raindrops cause some of the weedkiller to be carried on to the edges of the lawn, which may thereby be damaged and spoiled for months. L-section and other raised kerb units are also used as edgings to lawns and flower beds, for the construction

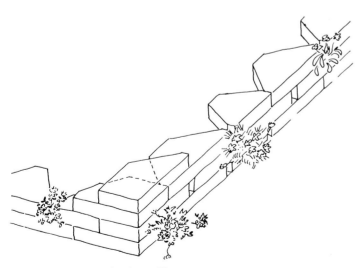

Danish plant blocks for dry walling

Small plants grow very well in the wall pockets *(see p.44)*

35

Garden wall of rammed concrete

In-situ concrete wall. The pattern was formed by triangular panels fixed to the inside of the formwork. The recessed bays have been painted in a dark colour

of small playing areas containing sand, and as surrounds to ponds or fountains.

The border separating a lawn from a gravel path may also be formed by slabs laid down in the reclining position. These slabs must be made substantially thicker than normal paving slabs, however. Their advantage is that, when the lawn is being mown, one wheel of the mowing machine can travel on the edging slabs, so that the tedious work of trimming the edges of the lawn is obviated. Another arrangement is to use vertical kerbs in combination with horizontal slabs functioning as a channel along the path or roadway. If channel units are installed, adequate arrangements for water discharge at suitable points should be provided. Paths and roads paved with precast concrete slabs require no kerbs or channels. The slabs are laid to a crossfall of 1–2 per cent and flush with the level of the ground. Rainwater is thus discharged uniformly to the adjacent lawns or planted areas.

Garden walls

Walls of various types and sizes are recurrent features in garden planning. Besides having a functional purpose, they can, with suitable design and the right construction materials, be very attractive ornamental features. Retaining walls are often used to overcome differences in level in gardens or to form horizontal areas for terraces or other purposes. Especially

in small gardens, retaining walls are preferable to earth slopes. As in the case of pavings, garden walls may be constructed from natural stone blocks or from precast concrete (more particularly: cast stone).

Natural stone has been the traditional wall construction material, as it forms a very suitable transition between the plants and the soil. Alternatively, cast stone blocks can very appropriately be used for the purpose, especially if this material is used also for other features in the garden. Familiarity with natural stone and the desire to imitate it as closely as possible in concrete, however, has sometimes resulted in disagreeable attempts to reproduce tooled finishes which are appropriate only to the natural material (bush hammering, etc.) or indeed to produce fake joints as integral features cast with the slabs.

What interesting possibilities are available when the aesthetic potentialities inherent in the concrete itself are utilized was demonstrated by the 'Nattermauer' ('snakeskin wall') exhibited by the landscape gardening consultants Günther Schulze and Joachim Winkler at the Federal Garden Show in Cologne. Cast stone units, 60 cm (24 in) long and up to 18 cm (7 in) high, were used to build a 'dry' masonry wall. These units were coloured in various shades of greyish blue, thus producing a striking 'snakeskin' pattern.

By utilizing trapezoidal and triangular shapes, wall building

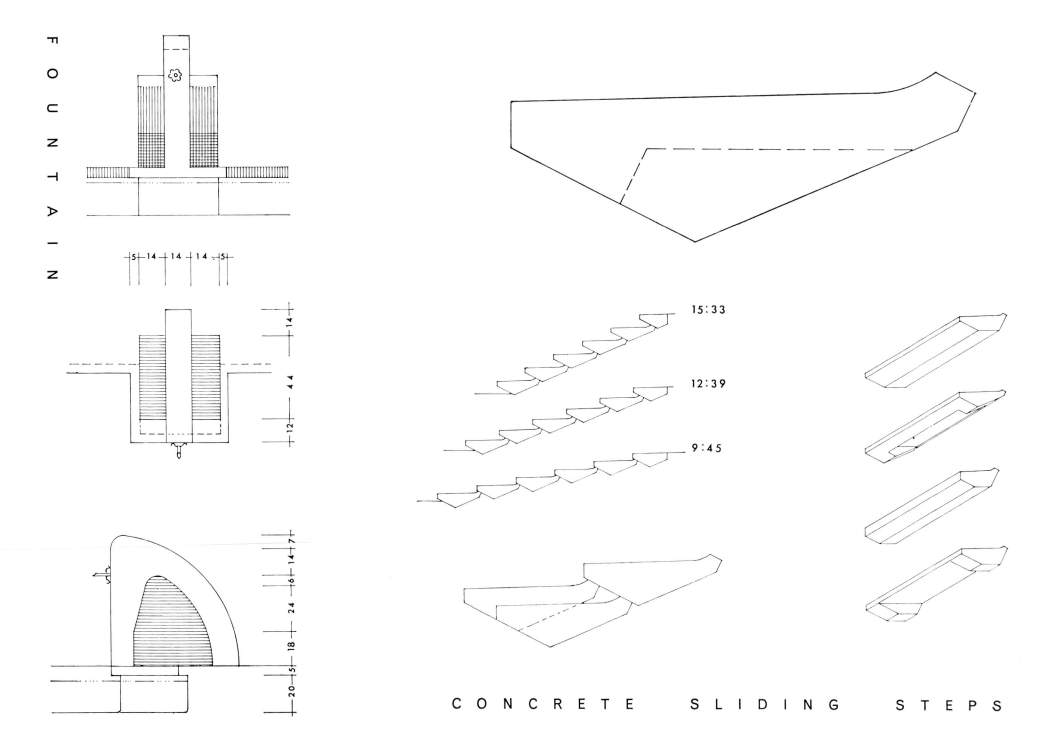

F O U N T A I N

15:33

12:39

9:45

C O N C R E T E   S L I D I N G   S T E P S

PLAYCORNER

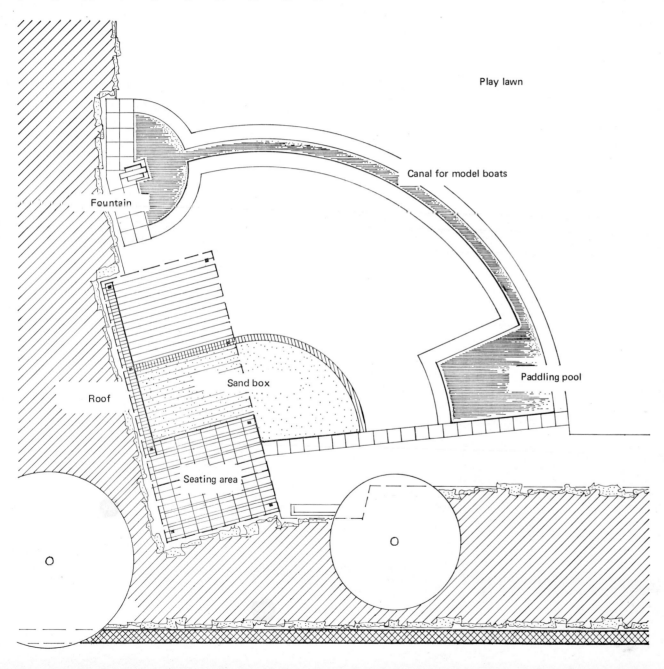

Play lawn

Canal for model boats

Fountain

Paddling pool

Roof

Sand box

Seating area

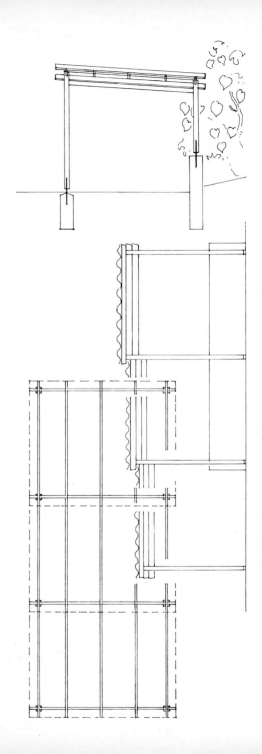

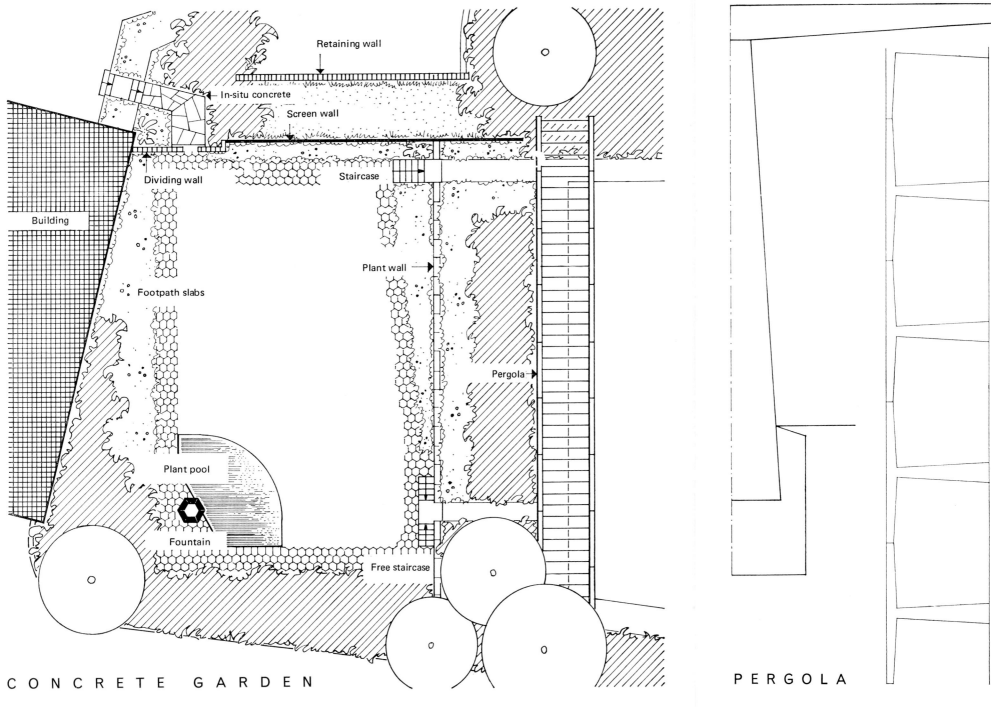

Retaining wall

In-situ concrete

Screen wall

Staircase

Dividing wall

Building

Plant wall

Footpath slabs

Pergola

Plant pool

Fountain

Free staircase

C O N C R E T E   G A R D E N

P E R G O L A

C**

FOUNTAIN

PLANT POOL

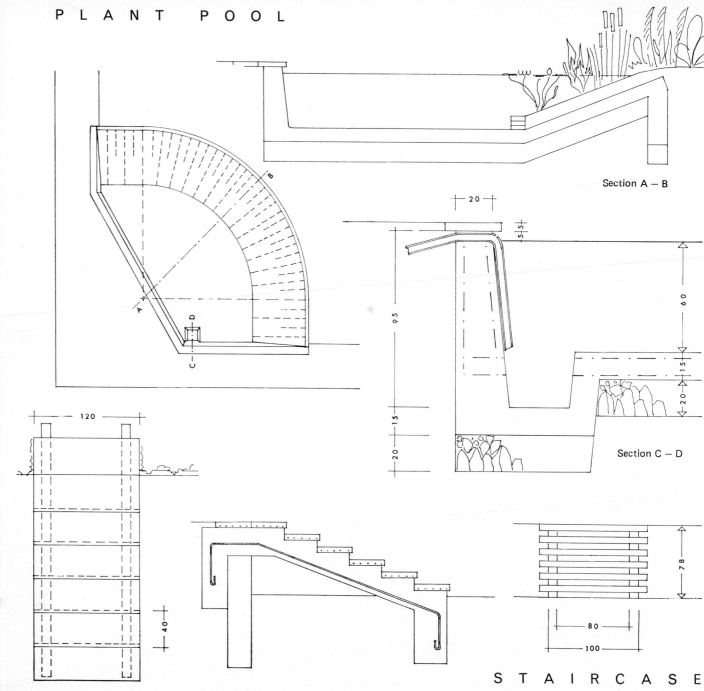

Section A – B

Section C – D

STAIRCASE

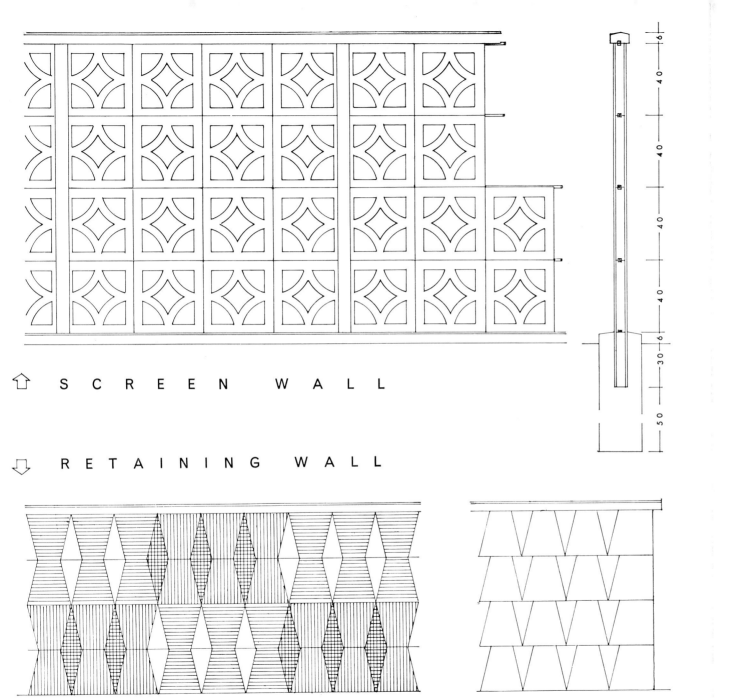

⬆ S C R E E N   W A L L

⬇ R E T A I N I N G   W A L L

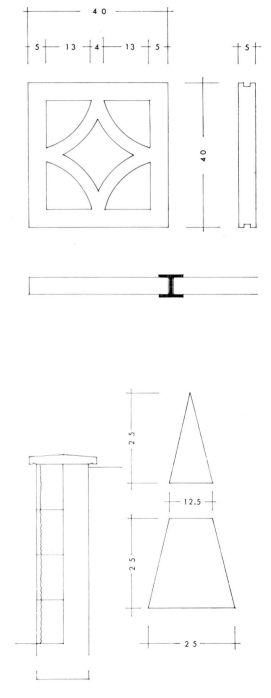

DIVIDING WALL

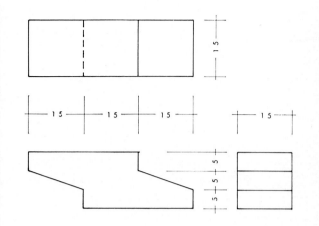

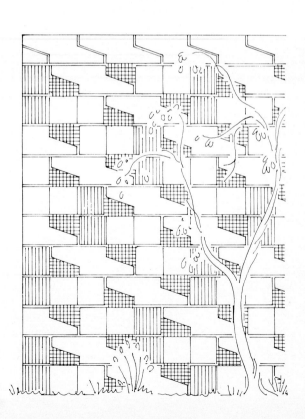

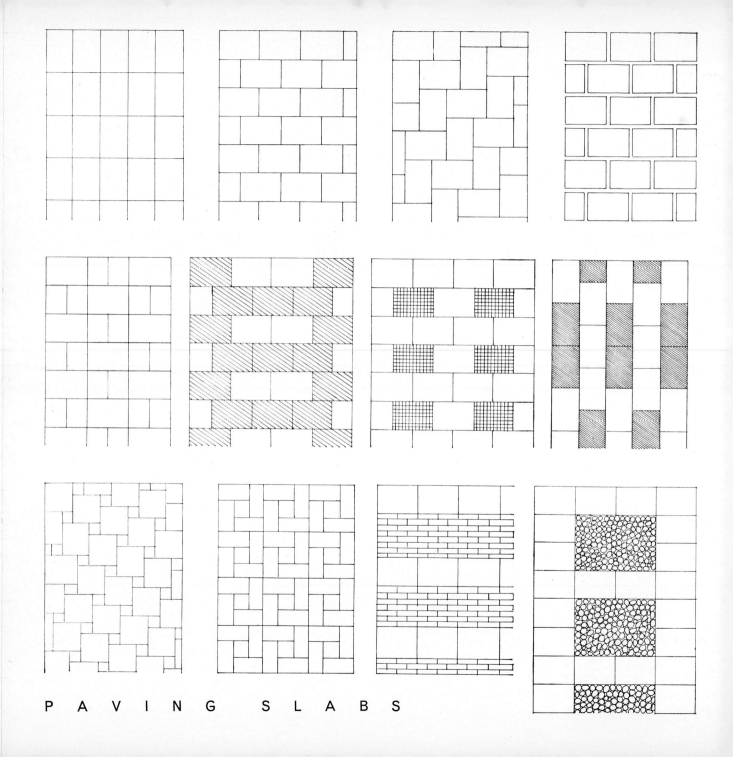

PAVING SLABS

In-situ concrete retaining walls and steps with exposed aggregate finish

Low retaining walls and steps with exposed aggregate finish

blocks have been produced which can be assembled in a great variety of patterns. Either the triangles are placed upon the trapeziums or the trapeziums and triangles alternate with one another. The wall can be further enlivened by alternation of the colours of the blocks, and further variety can be introduced by the application of different concrete surface finishes. A striking feature of the wall exhibited was its 'weather sensitivity': its colour scheme varied with the humidity of the atmosphere. After a time, the user of these wall building blocks gets to know their colour variations and can adjust himself to them.

Of course, other types of precast concrete blocks can suitably be used for wall construction. The desired rough surfaces are obtained by means of special treatments. The most usual method is by splitting pressed concrete blocks into halves; the fracture face of each half forms the external surface of the wall. In such split blocks the aggregate particles are exposed in ever varying patterns. These blocks must of course be coloured through and through. Exposed aggregate finishes and rough textures can also be obtained by methods similar to those already described for paving slabs.

Screen walls and dividing walls can very advantageously be constructed from cast stone blocks. Blocks of special shape (often pierced) and produced with skilled workmanship are used for these structures. These walls are characterized by having numerous apertures, arranged in a pleasing pattern, through which breezes can blow and which permit glimpses of what is on the other side of the wall, and yet provide some degree of privacy. With such walls a garden can be divided into separate areas without completely separating them as a solid wall would do. Ornamental effects are obtained by varied construction and alternating arrangement of the constructional elements. Delicate spots of colour and subdued light fall on plants growing behind the wall. The force of winds is broken so that they become pleasant breezes blowing through the spaces thus enclosed. These specially shaped and/or pierced screen wall blocks add an attractive new feature to landscape gardening in that they enable small enclosures to be formed within the large garden.

Ornamental screen wall blocks made with grey or white cement are manufactured in a variety of shapes and in excellent quality by precast concrete works. The blocks are usually 40 cm ($15\frac{3}{4}$ in) wide, 40 cm ($15\frac{3}{4}$ in) high and 10 cm (4 in) thick and are formed with holes of different shapes and sizes. Other wall units used for similar purposes are not pierced by holes, but can be assembled to form walls with numerous openings in them, e.g., cross-shaped members or elongated units which can be built up to form flattened honeycomb patterns. Sometimes the openings can be glazed. Pierced screen walls can be constructed with one such type of block or with a combination of two or three types.

These carefully constructed walls are tending to supersede the traditional dry stone walls, often covered with plants. The aesthetic effect of the shapes usually outweighs the desire to cover up the wall with creepers and other vegetation. The plain smooth-faced concrete block wall may, however, be found somewhat tame or monotonous. Such wall faces can be given greater interest and variety by providing them with recesses or pockets in which plants can be rooted or by the inclusion of projecting stones to provide a foothold for rock-growing plants. In Denmark, a country where suitable natural stone is scarce, precast concrete has long been used for the construction of dry walling composed of rectangular and trapezoidal blocks. The principal requirement is that plants which are to grow on or in such a wall should be able to root properly in the earth behind it. This is fulfilled by the use of trapezoidal blocks ('plant blocks', as they are called in Denmark).

To build a simple 'planting wall' of cast stone blocks, three wooden moulds were constructed from nailed boards: one large rectangle, one rectangle of the same length but only half the width, and one large rectangle minus a quarter of its area. Using the blocks which had been made in these moulds, the wall was so constructed that a certain number of holes extended right through it in a particular pattern. The blocks themselves consisted of concrete in several shades of brown. Inserted in each of the holes was a small slab which protruded a few centimetres from the front of the wall. Earth was placed on these protruding slabs, and small ornamental shrubs were planted in it. All these plants developed excellently, and their flowers showed to advantage against the neutral background colour of the wall. The moulds in which the blocks were cast were of rather rough-and-ready construction, so that the joints between the blocks did not appear too precise and neat.

There are, of course, many other possible ways of building concrete walls that will provide a base for the growth of plants. Pockets or recesses for plants can be formed with sections of asbestos cement pipes which are inserted into the bonding pattern of many types of wall construction blocks. Also, blocks moulded with cavities may be employed for modestly conceived 'planting walls'.

In the case of larger and higher walls which are to serve as enclosures it is possible to obtain variety and a distinctive character by the use of carefully constructed formwork comprising special panels or with strips (to form imprints in the concrete) fixed to the inner face thereof. It will seldom be necessary entirely to surround a garden with such a wall. Usually it will suffice to build the wall only in one direction or along part of the perimeter. These walls should be built on foundations which extend to below the frost penetration depth and which should moreover be reinforced. Expansion joints are necessary at intervals of about 10 m (30–35 ft).

The exhibits at the Federal Garden Show in Cologne included a concrete wall whose front face had, by means of appropriate inserts in the formwork, been given a distinctive pattern which had been accentuated by painting in different colours. The wall face can be enlivened by nailing blocks or slabs of plastic to the inside of the formwork, or by exposing the aggregate particles.

If the interstices between the component elements in an ornamental wall are increased in size, a pierced screen effect is obtained, and if the apertures are made still larger, the wall will resemble an open-work fence. At one exhibition the author saw a fence of slender concrete planks so installed as to produce the effect of Venetian blinds. The oblique setting of the planks prevented direct see-through, but the wide apertures between them allowed light and air to pass.

Steps

It is often necessary to build steps in gardens. Besides their purely functional purpose – to overcome differences in height conveniently – they afford opportunities of introducing attractive features into the garden.

Unfortunately, it is often difficult to procure steps which harmonize with the colours of the slabs used on the paths, terraces and other paved areas. In most cases the only solution will be to employ steps consisting of such paving slabs forming the treads, in combination with separate units for the risers. Ordinary paving slabs can be used for the purpose, but in that case the coloured facing layer or the surface finish should be continued on to the front edges of the slabs serving as treads. Slabs which are coloured through and through are more suitable here. If the steps are of such width as to require several slabs side by side, the joints in the successive steps should be staggered. If the joints coincided, an unfavourable visual effect would result, as though the flight of steps were liable to break apart.

In the absence of block steps or special tread slabs which harmonize with the paving slabs and walling blocks it may be a good idea to use steps or slabs made with white cement. Although such steps stand out prominently from their surroundings, this is not inappropriate for such important functional features.

Modern angular shapes are encountered in slab-type steps which are laid on two stringer members or, alternatively, on one central stringer (if the individual steps are strong enough). Cantilevered slabs which at one end are built into a wall can

Cantilevered steps fixed into wall at one end

Sliding steps being installed

also provide an attractive solution for garden staircases, but they require very careful reinforcement and good insertion into the blockwork bond of the wall.

More durable, and therefore preferable for garden use, are block-type (monolithic) steps. Particular care must be given to the design of the front faces of such steps, which should be slightly convex or formed with a slight break.

Block-type steps all suffer from the disadvantage that the height of the step and the width of the tread normally cannot be varied. On the other hand, with built-up steps composed of separate units for the treads and risers, respectively, these dimensions can easily be varied within certain limits.

The manufacture and stocking of large quantities of block-type steps for landscape gardening purposes has hitherto not proved profitable, because the differences in level to be overcome vary from one job to another, requiring different step heights and correspondingly different widths of the steps. Also, slopes cannot always be adjusted to the pitch of the steps. In such circumstances the staircase will either be recessed deeply into the slope or will protrude objectionably above it. For this reason it is often preferable to use built-up steps whose riser and tread widths can more readily be adapted to the requirements of any particular situation. On the other hand, the block-type step has the advantage of greater durability, being more resistant to destructive atmospheric influences, besides being easier to install. Attempts have therefore been made to develop a type of step having a variable height, while for each height ('rise') the appropriate

tread width ('going') is automatically available, i.e., without necessitating any cutting or trimming of the steps. The solution is provided by block-type steps of the 'sliding' type, which can be slid (displaced) in relation to one another along the two parallel surfaces with which they are provided. In this way the ratio of rise to going can be kept constant. For garden steps this ratio can suitably be within the range from 10:35 to 10:43, corresponding to the formula commonly employed (in Germany): $2R + G = 63$ cm (25 in), where $R =$ rise and $G =$ going. For steps which give access to a garden from a house, a terrace or a forecourt the ratio should preferably be 13:37, i.e., the steps should have a rise of 13 cm ($5\frac{1}{4}$ in), while the going should be 37 cm ($14\frac{1}{2}$ in). The maximum rise acceptable for garden steps is 17 cm ($6\frac{3}{4}$ in), which corresponds – according to the formula – to a going of 29 cm ($11\frac{1}{2}$ in).

With the special 'sliding' variable steps, as envisaged above, it is possible to obtain any rise-to-going ratio within the range from 8:47 to 17:29. Lower steps can be constructed from blocks formed with recesses, in which case the 'sliding' for adjustment is confined to surfaces provided at the ends of the steps. For rises exceeding 15 cm (6 in) only the solid type of step can be employed, otherwise the individual step cannot obtain adequate support in the ground.

Solid block steps of this adjustable kind have been installed in the 'Monrepos' garden at Geisenheim, Germany. They were cast in home-made open wooden moulds. In the interests of durability it is essential to use a favourably graded aggregate mixture and to apply efficient mixing and careful compaction of the concrete.

Pergolas

A pergola is a kind of arbour or open pavilion covered with roses or climbing plants and performing a space-controlling function, especially in the smaller garden. It may serve as a dividing or separating feature, but also as a means of inter-connecting different parts of a garden. Depending on its purpose and the landscape gardener's intentions, the pergola may have a dense and relatively closed or, alternatively, a more open and widely spaced form of construction. The main function of the pergola is to form a suitable base for climbing plants such as clematis, wistaria, climbing roses, certain vari-eties of honeysuckle, and many others.

As the name suggests, the pergola has been introduced from southern climes. Its simple original form is sometimes still encountered on the sunny slopes of Italian vineyards. Plain slender stone columns, split off from a slab of granite or gneiss, are set upright as monoliths, serving to support a rustic framework of oak or chestnut logs. The vines creep up these frameworks; the bunches of grapes hang protected under the foliage. From the vineyards the pergola spread to the gardens of the Italian country estates and thence to gardens all over the world.

Closest to the original primitive form are pergolas whose columns or posts are monoliths, i.e., each consisting of a single piece of stone. At the top of each column a sharp-edged notch is formed in which the rough round timbers of the top framework are simply laid without any positive means of connection. More carefully constructed pergolas have con-crete columns which support squared wooden beams which in turn carry wooden cross-members of smaller section. De-pending on whether a closed pergola producing a roofed-in effect or a more open framework for climbing plants is desired, the main beams are placed longitudinally, while the cross-members can be spaced as closely as may be desired, or alternatively – for constructing the open type of pergola – the cross-members serve as the supporting elements for the longitudinal beams, which are placed over them.

Besides stone, concrete can suitably be used for the supporting columns. These may be of polygonal – octagonal (8-sided) or dodecagonal (10-sided) cross-section and have special surface finishes, e.g. exposed aggregate. Precast concrete lighting columns can be employed for the purpose.

Not only the columns but also the beams of a pergola may be of concrete, in which case it is a truly concrete structure. The 'roof' framework for the climbing plants may, however, consist of other materials, e.g., round or rectangular metal tubes, or asbestos cement tubes.

Of course, the pergola columns may be constructed of pre-cast concrete masonry. This calls for careful workmanship. Each masonry column, composed of blocks, should be sur-mounted by a capping slab on which the wooden beams can be laid. In order to avoid direct contact between the slab and the wood, it is advisable to interpose a sheet of lead between them or to provide the capping slab with a special cramp-iron to serve as a bearing for the woodwork. However, this point where iron, concrete and rainwater may interact is rather a critical point, which can best be avoided by using other materials.

Excellent and yet relatively cheap pergola columns can be constructed by placing lengths of concrete pipe one upon the other to obtain the desired height and then filling them with lean concrete. At the top of each column a circular or square capping slab is installed. The unattractive grey colour of the concrete can be concealed under a coat of special paint.

Concrete pergola. The columns are steel tubes; the panels at the base are of asbestos cement. Some of the bays have a fabric mesh infilling to support climbing plants

Concrete pergola with climbing roses

Different pipe diameters can be employed for the columns, depending on the size of the garden and of the pergola.

Climbing plants are made to grow up the columns. Roses, for example, require some extra support. On reaching the top of the columns, the plants spread out over the 'roof' framework. Wooden trellises, tubular latticework or fabric mesh mats may be mounted between pairs of adjacent columns and thus serve as supports for climbing plants.

Pergolas provide an excellent means of enhancing the amenities of any garden, and with concrete they can be particularly attractive structures.

Ponds and pools

Hardly any other garden planning feature offers so many fascinating possibilities as water does. There is nothing like water for adding life and interest to any scene; it is attractive and refreshing; it creates focal points of interest, without presenting any obstruction to the wandering gaze and concealing any of the scenery beyond it. In warm weather, water, whether in a tranquil pool or in lively streaming motion, exercises an appreciable cooling effect on account of the evaporation that takes place. The continual movements of its surface, the gleaming and flashing of even the tiniest ripples, and the gentle lapping or murmur of the water at the inlet to the pool produce a mysterious and dreamlike atmosphere. Water greatly enriches the garden. It is the garden's eye and thus forms part of its very soul.

The actual purpose or function of the water is not necessarily of major importance with regard to its aesthetic effect. Ponds for trout culture or pools for water-lilies in a special water garden exercise the same lively attraction as does the carefully constructed spring in a garden simulating natural scenery or the reflecting pool of the modern house. Whether formal ponds of geometrically regular shape or free-shaped expanses of water are constructed, they never fail to exercise a distinctive charm. Of course, many real and useful functions have been devised for water in the garden: the bathing pool for the whole family's recreation, the plant pond for the lover of aquatic botanical treasures, the simple reflecting pool, and last but not least the children's paddling pool. These various types of ponds and pools have all been extensively dealt with in books and periodical literature. The present author's object is simply to give some indications and suggestions.

To fulfil all the requirements that have been mentioned is possible only because we have an extremely adaptable and versatile material – concrete – at our disposal for the construction of these garden features. It is nowadays indeed possible to construct watertight pools with other materials, such as bitumen or plastic sheeting; but the greatest scope and the best guarantee for durability are afforded by concrete when this material is used expertly.

Swimming pools are to be classed among the larger structures of this general category. The need for them, and the recreational value they offer, call for no comment. The possibility of

Small swimming pool in a private garden

L-shaped plant pool

Private swimming pool adjacent to terrace paved with precast concrete slabs

Water-lilies on a dark water surface

bathing at any time and at any temperature in a heated pool in the privacy of one's own garden have made the swimming pool an important and much sought-after amenity. It should be pointed out, however, that pools are a constant source of danger to children who cannot swim. Like their elders, children are greatly attracted by water, and there is hardly anything they enjoy better than playing near and with water.

In the case of the plant pool the main emphasis is on the cultivation of aquatic plants. Its purpose is to recreate or 'capture' an interesting piece of nature, a plant community which is hardly to be found in the wild state. It is important to note that the plant pool, too, should comprise an area of open water to reflect the sky. At least one-third of the pool's surface in its final state should be free from plants.

The various possible planting arrangements – free planting in a bed of earth on the bottom, plants rooted in tubs or baskets placed in the pool, or rooted in recesses formed in the pool – have been described elsewhere. From the viewpoint of tending the plants and arranging them, it is preferable to have them growing in tubs. However, this means foregoing the possibility of many surprising and particularly interesting observations.

Nowadays it is considered desirable to locate a shallow pool presenting a calm sheet of water close to the house, beside a terrace or in front of large low-placed windows. The water pleasingly reflects the architectural features and the adjacent vegetation, thus constituting a charming revival of the old reflecting pools which were a favourite ornamental device in

Innocent joy in a paddling pool

Polygonal fountain basin as a terminal feature on a garden terrace

baroque gardens. To obtain good reflections, the concrete bottom and sides of the pool should be given a black coating of bitumen of a type which is compatible with plant life. Suitable bituminous compounds for the purpose have been developed for use in silos and drinking-water tanks.

Pools for cascades, fountains, etc. can also advantageously be constructed of concrete. Attractive effects are obtainable by the use of ornamental colours, mosaic-type surface finishes or exposed aggregates. To enable aquatic plants to grow in a shallow pool, they may be planted in concrete tubs which are recessed below the bottom of the pool at a number of points. Larger pools and ponds should be provided with steel reinforcement. If the pool exceeds a certain size – about 6 m (20 ft) – it becomes necessary to provide expansion joints. A joint of this kind has to be made watertight with a suitable sealing compound or a water-stop. The concreting operations should be executed in accordance with certain rules for obtaining watertight concrete. Besides, it may be advantageous to use a waterproofing agent as an admixture to the cement rendering or surfacing applied to the concrete.

Fountains

Fountains are another group of garden structures making use of water as an ornamental feature. Whereas formerly it was hardly possible, for reasons of material and labour, to build large fountains to suit the garden owners' individual ideas, nowadays such wishes can indeed be fulfilled. With concrete construction, even if white cement and specially selected aggregates are employed, the cost of the materials and the direct cost of building the fountain scarcely play a significant part. But a complex mould or some rather elaborate formwork

Swimming pool in a private garden: edge coping and terrace paving have exposed aggregate finish

51

Small fountain constructed in two-coloured concrete

The particular fountain basin envisaged in this example is about 1·60 m (5 ft 3 in) wide and 0·47 m (1 ft 6½ in) high, supported on a low pedestal 0·60 m (1 ft 11½ in) in diameter. The most time-consuming part of the operation consists in making the mould. In order to obtain smooth surfaces and sharp arrises, the mould should be constructed of strong 8 mm ($\frac{5}{16}$ in) plywood. Each panel should be additionally strengthened by laths fixed to the outside; these laths also serve to join the panels together by means of screws. All the internal surfaces of the mould should be carefully smoothed and any cracks or cavities sealed with a filler. They should then be given a coating of colourless varnish. Next, the basin mould is placed on the mould or formwork for the pedestal and is carefully adjusted to the correct level. Additional props should be inserted under the cantilevering basin mould on all sides.

When the reinforcement has been installed in the mould, the pedestal and basin are concreted together, in one continuous operation taking several hours to carry out. White cement should be used, and to make the concrete watertight, particularly good grading of the aggregates is essential. The mix should contain 350 kg of cement per cubic metre of concrete (600 lb per cubic yard) and be of feebly plastic consistency.

is needed, which may make the job expensive. The spare-time gardener may, however, find it a rewarding task for the winter months to construct his own formwork for the fountain, which he may have planned as a basin, bowl or tank. This does, however, call for some skill in working with wood and for careful consideration of how to construct the formwork and cast the concrete. Industrial manufacture of such moulds or formwork is seldom economically feasible, the more so as they are generally used for one job only. As a rule they must therefore be individual purpose-made structures.

The following example outlines the operations in constructing a simple fountain. The fountain basin, supported on a low pedestal, is to be located in a part of the garden with paving composed of hexagonal precast concrete slabs in shades of yellow and brown. The basin will likewise be hexagonal in shape. In designing such a structure it is necessary always to give due consideration to the distinctive qualities of the material. In order not to make the formwork too difficult to construct, it is preferable to use simple compact shapes: polyhedral structures bounded by straight or slightly curved lines. Of course, concrete can be cast into more elaborate shapes in appropriately constructed moulds which can produce complex hollow features, relief-like ornamental detail or intricate latticework. The cost of such formwork is so high, however, that the economic advantage of using concrete as the construction material is largely cancelled out.

Setting up the formwork

Reinforcement, overflow and inlet pipe have been installed

The mould being filled with concrete

The inner part of the mould has been removed; props continue to support the outer mould

This will ensure that all parts of the mould will be properly filled. It is important to achieve good compaction by tamping and punning.

After a few days the sides of the mould can be removed, but the props under the basin and the bottom formwork should be left in position for some time longer. After removal of the mould comes the important operation of curing the concrete. This consists in carefully protecting the concrete from sun and wind, so as to prevent excessively rapid drying, and in keeping the concrete constantly moist for two weeks. The basin should be filled with water immediately after the formwork has been removed.

At the centre of the basin is an overflow pipe which keeps the water level constant at 5 cm (2 in) below the edge. Concentrically within the overflow pipe is the inlet pipe which divides into two branches directly above the mouth of the overflow. These branches rise to a height of 80 cm (2 ft 7½ in) above the top of the basin and terminate in a pair of nozzles facing in opposite directions. A vertical disc is mounted between the nozzles, and the two jets of water issuing from them produce an attractive continually changing pattern.

In winter the basin is emptied and covered with a wooden cover, which serves as a bird feeding table. The two branch pipes are removed and can be replaced by a screwed-on length of pipe carrying a wire framework which supports a thatched roof to protect the bird table.

The construction of this fountain has been described in some detail in order also to bring out the difficulties and to call attention to the manual skills required. When planning to build a structure of this kind, it should always be borne in mind that simple moulds, clear-cut outlines, and cavities without complex shapes will make the work a good deal easier. All the usual concrete surface finishing techniques, such as colouring the concrete, exposing the aggregate particles, etc., can additionally be applied, if so desired.

Bird baths may be regarded as miniature ornamental basins, which can be made in a variety of shapes, such as a slab with a shallow depression, a flat dish, or a low bowl embellished with ornamental features. In gardens to which prowling cats have access it is advisable to mount the bird bath well above ground level. For instance, a flat dish may be mounted on the top of a thin tubular support, or the bath may consist of a waist-high concrete block provided with a shallow depression at the top and with delicate relief-like moulded features on its sides.

White concrete fountain

The disc mounted between the two nozzles

Play corners

Children should always have access to a garden as a place to grow up in. With only a little guidance they learn to observe, recognize and understand many things that they will later be taught in an abstract and much less easy-to-understand form at school. Playing in the fresh air in a garden, out of harm's way and safe from the perils of the street, brings valuable enrichment to the child's world and welcome relief to the mother. In order to keep children under better control, it is advisable always to provide a small play corner in the garden – if possible, in a position where it can be properly supervised from the house. This play area need not be expensively equipped, but it should offer some simple facilities that will at least tempt any small child to stay and play there. It will, of course, not be possible thus to induce older children to confine their activities to this particular area; for them there will be the whole garden to romp and play in.

An indispensable feature of every play corner is a sand box. The most favourable form of construction is with rammed concrete walls which are rounded at the top and flush with the general ground level. The 'box' or 'pit' should be at least 40 cm (1 ft 4 in) and preferably 60 cm (2 ft) deep; otherwise the children will be frustrated when, in their burrowing operations, they encouter the hard bottom too soon. The bottom may be of concrete. It may adequately consist of simple rectangular footway slabs laid in close contact with one another on a bed of sand. Thus the two requirements applicable to the bottom of a children's sand box are fulfilled: a suitable base for shovelling when it becomes necessary to change the sand, and good permeability to let surface water drain away.

There should be no sharp angles and corners, nor any complex profiles. Frequently a sand box is built above ground level, but unless the soil conditions necessitate this, it is preferable to recess it into the ground: the children find this more exciting and more satisfying to play in. The sand box can then also serve as a jumping pit and be used for all sorts of running and chasing games. A play table may also be an advantageous feature. It consists of a smooth row of precast concrete slabs on which sand 'cakes' can be baked and which can also serve as a parking area for the toy cars and trucks that are an inseparable feature of playing with sand.

A good idea is to cover half the sand box with a roof, thus giving the children a choice of playing in the sun or in the shade; and they will be able to go on playing even in light rain. A simple and fairly inexpensive solution is provided by a

The delights of the sand box

A play sculpture with a slide on the Killesberg at Stuttgart

timber framework, open on all sides and supporting a roof made of corrugated asbestos cement or plastic sheets.

If a paddling pool can be included, this will of course be an added source of delight to the children and a great asset to the play corner. However, the water and sand should be kept well apart.

Another very popular feature is a scribbling wall. It provides an opportunity for all sorts of first attempts at artistic creation or shaky experiments in scrawling the sort of illegible hieroglyphics in which some children give expression to their early experience of life. Later they will indulge in more serious activities of writing and drawing, culminating in more or less successful attempts at caricaturing everyone and everything around them. Children may even use the wall for climbing and jumping, as the photograph on page 56 shows. This wall

Concrete sculpture : cave and slide in a children's playground at Stockholm

The scribbling wall being used as a jumping-off wall

was constructed as a free-standing structure of unreinforced rammed concrete. Initially it was given a white cement rendering as a suitable surface to receive the children's graffiti; at a later stage, this surface was given a coating of black bitumen. The animal pictures seen in the photograph were cut-out shapes which were glued to the wall before the bitumen was applied.

Vases and bowls

Concrete is an excellent and inexpensive material for making ornamental vases and bowls of all kinds, with regular or irregular shapes, with or without reinforcement. And this brings us back to Monier, who started it all by putting iron reinforcement in his plant tubs. It is indeed amazing that a mere sideline of landscape gardening — making tubs, vases and bowls for plants — was to become the starting point of a revolutionary and world-wide development in the whole art and science of construction.

Present-day methods of making concrete garden vases are illustrated by the following examples.

Concrete sculpture in a garden

Concrete vase coloured to harmonize with red sandstone

A large asymmetrically shaped vase was constructed by taking strong wire netting and tying it in the shape of the future vase. A very stiff and rich concrete mix was applied to the netting by hand and patted on. The last layer of concrete contained a red pigment, so that the finished vase harmonized with the red sandstone masonry on which it was placed.

Another vase was constructed by a different method. The external outline of the vase was drawn on a thin sheet of building board, which was then cut out to form a template. A pile of loam or clay was placed on the floor of the workshop and rammed so as to give it roughly the shape of the future vase. Finally, an iron bar was stuck in the middle of the heap. The template, in a position corresponding to having the bottom of the vase upwards and the mouth down at floor level, was attached to the iron bar. By constantly rotating the template the loam core was gradually worked to the correct shape. Next, an approximately 4 cm (1½ in) thick casing of concrete was applied to the core. Here again the concrete mix had to be of very stiff consistency. The template was then moved 4 cm (1½ in) outwards and was used to work the

Cheerful concrete sculpture in a school garden

Austere concrete shapes soften by the luxuriant splendour of vegetation

surface of the concrete to the correct shape. After the concrete had hardened, the vase was carefully turned, i.e., placed right way up, and the loam core scraped out. Finally, the internal surface of the vase was coated with a bitumen emulsion compatible with plants.

Of course, vases of all kinds can also be cast in conventional moulds; but such moulds are by no means cheap to construct.

The term 'mobile garden' has been applied to hollow precast concrete units of hexagonal shape on plan and open at top and bottom. These units can be assembled into structures varying in size and height. They can be installed in precincts,

in paved courtyards, or on roof terraces, and filled with earth in which plants can grow. Should the units no longer be required, they can be removed at any time.

Gardens are modern man's last refuge – a quiet place where he can withdraw for undisturbed enjoyment of the open air, for the fulfilment of many desires and favourite pursuits, and for being in contact with nature. As a means of establishing an ordered pattern, of providing amenities that add to the comfort and pleasure of being in the garden, and of creating attractive and interesting ornamental features, concrete shows itself to be an excellent aid in modern landscape gardening.

The purpose of these instructions is to give the layman some guidance in making concrete for simple components and structures such as are used in gardens. Difficult and more heavily loaded structural members should not, however, be constructed as do-it-yourself jobs, but should always be entrusted to specialist firms and skilled workmen.

Hardened concrete is an artificial stone which is produced by mixing cement, aggregates and water in suitable quantitative proportions.

Cement

In various countries of Continental Europe cement is supplied in bags containing 50 kg; for all practical purposes this quantity is equivalent to the standard 1 cwt (112 lb) bag in which cement is supplied in Britain.

The cement normally used for construction work in the garden (and indeed for most other purposes) is Portland cement, which (in Britain) is available in two main types: ordinary and rapid-hardening. In general, ordinary Portland cement is suitable for the type of work with which this book is concerned. Another type of cement which can be used for general purposes and whose properties are mainly similar to those of ordinary Portland cement is Portland blastfurnace cement. This is a mixture composed of about two-thirds of pulverized blastfurnace slag and one-third of Portland cement.

Before use, cement should be kept carefully protected from moisture. It is advisable not to order more bags from the supplier than will be used immediately. If the cement has to be stored, however, the bags should be placed on a platform of boards resting on battens in a dry enclosed space. The bags should not touch the floor or the walls of the latter.

Aggregates

The usual aggregates for making concrete are sand and gravel. Crushed stone aggregates are sometimes also used. Sand and gravel are 'natural' aggregates, being excavated from pits and river beds; they have rounded particles. Crushed stone aggregates (crushed stone sand, chippings, broken stone), which are produced from quarried stone by mechanical crushing and are in this sense 'artificial' products, have angular particles. Because of this latter fact, crushed stone aggregates in a concrete mix require more water to obtain the necessary workability than natural aggregates do.

The aggregates used in the mix should be suitably graded, i.e., they should consist of particles of various sizes, so proportioned that the smaller particles will more or less fill the cavities between the larger ones. This will help to produce dense strong concrete. For our purpose the following grading may be recommended: 50 per cent of the particles over 7 mm (approx. $\frac{1}{4}$ in) and 50 per cent under 7 mm in size; of the latter, more than half should consist of sand with a particle size of less than 3 mm (approx. $\frac{1}{8}$ in).*

The upper size limit of the aggregate particles that can be used in the mix will depend on the dimensions of the structure to be built. As a general rule, the largest particle size should not exceed about one-fifth of the least dimension of the structure or component which has to be concreted.

Aggregates contaminated with dirt should not be used, as the strength of the concrete would thereby be impaired and damage might be caused to the structure. Such contaminating substances may be: earth, loam, coal grit or remains of vegetable matter. Unwashed aggregates which are delivered to the job site should therefore always be examined to make sure that they are free from contamination.

Additives may be introduced into the concrete for specific purposes — e.g., waterproofers to make the concrete impermeable to water, air-entraining agents to improve its frost resistance, or retarders to delay the setting (this can be useful at construction joints: when a retarder is added to the last batch of concrete placed before work is interrupted, the setting of this concrete can thus be delayed for several hours, so that concreting can then be resumed without requiring any special precautions at the joint). The effect of the additive, and the correct amount to use, should be established by means of preliminary tests.

Water

The amount of mixing water used is of great importance with regard to the strength and workability of the concrete. According as more water is added, the concrete becomes more workable, i.e., easier to place and to compact, but the lower will be the strength of the hardened concrete. A rough test for

---

* It is not possible to give exact practical equivalents of the metric dimensions. Readers will find helpful and simply presented information on how to make concrete in some of the publications of the Cement and Concrete Association, 52 Grosvenor Gardens, London, SW1.

judging the correct water content of a stiff concrete mix is that the cement paste from a pat of fresh concrete should remain adhering to the palm of the hand only when it is vigorously squeezed.

For reinforced concrete construction or for making watertight concrete a mix having a more plastic consistency should be used. Such a consistency can be achieved in conjunction with a fairly low water content of the mix (a high water content weakens the concrete!) only if very carefully graded aggregates are used. On small jobs, however, the facilities for doing this are generally lacking. As a rule, the only way to increase the workability in such circumstances is to add more water to the mix and offset its weakening effect by also increasing the cement content. The snag is that such 'rich' concrete tends to shrink more. To counteract this and to prevent the formation of shrinkage cracks, the surface of the young concrete must be protected from sun and wind and be kept damp for two to four weeks by covering it with wet sand or wet cloth (which should be sprayed with water at sufficiently frequent intervals).

The water to be used in mixing the concrete should be clean and free from harmful impurities. In certain cases water which looks clean may nevertheless be unsuitable for making concrete (e.g., industrial waste water).

Tools

Most of the tools required for simple concrete work belong to the gardener's normal equipment: shovel, rake, bucket, watering can with rose, hose, sieve, broom, rammer, trowel, wooden float, spirit-level, plumb-bob, as well as boards, nails and carpenter's tools for the construction of moulds and formwork. A hard firm base or a platform of boards on which the concrete can be mixed will also be needed.

Mixing concrete by hand

On small jobs the concrete is usually mixed by hand. This should be done on a non-absorptive level surface, preferably a large sheet of metal or a platform constructed of boards or some similar surface.

First, the gravel and sand mixture are placed on the working surface, and the measured quantity of cement is spread on top. The dry materials are then thoroughly mixed by turning them over with a shovel until a uniformly grey colour is obtained. Next, while mixing continues, water is added from a watering can fitted with a rose. Mixing the moistened materials should continue until the colour of the mix is uniform; mixing with the shovel should be assisted by turning the material over with a rake.

For more important work, which has to fulfil requirements of greater stringency as to the quality and more particularly the strength of the concrete, it is essential to use machine mixing and conform to certain other rules.

Mix proportions

On small jobs the traditional practice of batching the concrete by volumetric proportions of cement, aggregates and water is still widely adopted. (On larger and more important jobs, batching by weight is now almost universal.)

For minor structures quite a satisfactory concrete can be produced by using mix proportions of 1:5, i.e., one part of cement to five parts of aggregates. These quantities can be measured in a bucket, for example.

It should be noted that the cement content of the mix does not in itself provide a reliable indication of the quality of the concrete. The important criterion is how much water there is in relation to the amount of cement; this is called the water/cement ratio; the concrete will, generally speaking, develop higher strength according as this ratio is lower, and *vice versa*. From this point of view it is therefore good to use a mix with a low water/cement ratio, but there is a practical limit as to how low the ratio can be reduced, because if the mix is too 'dry', it becomes difficult to place and compact, so that cavities may remain in the concrete and its strength and density thus be impaired. On the other hand, with too much water the mix will be too 'wet', and the resulting concrete will likewise be deficient in strength.

A concrete which can suitably be used for most purposes where mechanical compaction with vibrators is not employed can be made by adding not more than 30 litres ($6\frac{1}{2}$ Imperial gallons) of water per bag of cement (112 lb). The required 'stiffness' of the mix can then be obtained by varying the overall quantity of the aggregates (sand + gravel) and/or the proportions of sand to gravel. For example, as a rough average, it can be said that about 200–250 litres ($7–8\frac{3}{4}$ cubic feet) of aggregates may be added to one bag of cement (112 lb) and 30 litres ($6\frac{1}{2}$ Imperial gallons) of water. The proportions of sand and gravel within this quantity of aggregates may be varied from 150 litres of sand ($5\frac{1}{4}$ cu ft) + 50 litres of gravel ($1\frac{3}{4}$ cu ft) to 100 litres of sand ($3\frac{1}{2}$ cu ft) + 150 litres of gravel ($5\frac{1}{4}$ cu ft).*

As a general rule, the mix should be of such consistency that it is sufficiently workable for the particular purpose for which it is to be employed, i.e., it should always be possible to place and compact it properly to produce a good dense concrete free from cavities. For a slender or narrow structure, or a structure containing reinforcement, it will generally be necessary to use a 'wetter' and therefore more plastic and workable mix than for a structure with ample dimensions in which the concrete can be easily placed and compacted.

Ready-mixed concrete

Before undertaking concrete work it is advisable to consider whether it would be advantageous to order ready-mixed concrete. Plants specializing in the manufacture and supply of concrete in special trucks to wherever it is required for *in-situ* use are nowadays to be found at nearly all centres of population in Western Europe and the United States.

Placing and compacting

On completion of mixing, the concrete should at once be placed in the formwork or mould. Formwork against which fair-faced (exposed) concrete will be formed should be treated with a release agent (mould oil) before concreting commences. If the concrete has to be conveyed some considerable distance between mixing and placing, care should be taken to ensure that segregation of its constituents does not occur on the way.

Stiff concrete should be deposited in the formwork in layers 15–20 cm (6–8 in) thick, and each layer should be energetically tamped until moisture appears at the surface of the concrete. Particularly good compaction should be applied at corners and at external surfaces. The rammed layer should be carefully roughened on top before the next layer is placed on it.

Structural parts which are interconnected should, as far as possible, all be concreted in one continuous operation. If interruptions in concreting cannot be avoided, the construction joints associated with the stopping and subsequent resumption should never be located at corners or in parts which will later be subjected to heavy loads. Before concreting is resumed, the face of the 'old' concrete at the joint should be roughened and given a coating of cement slurry.

Since concrete should be used as soon as possible after mixing, only so much concrete as is required for immediate use should be mixed.

Formwork removal and curing

Formwork should be removed when the concrete has had sufficient time to harden. Side panels of formwork can usually be stripped after three days; with rapid-hardening cement this period can be reduced to two days. Both before and after removal of the formwork the young concrete should be protected from sun and wind and be kept moist, as has already been described. Concreting in cold weather, more particularly during frost, calls for special precautions and should preferably be avoided, unless absolutely necessary.

The foregoing instructions for making and using concrete have been kept as simple as possible. For more detailed information, should that be required, the reader may consult the extensive literature on the subject or seek guidance from an organisation such as the Cement and Concrete Association, London.

---

* These are the author's figures. A commonly used general-purpose concrete is based on the 1:2:4 mix, containing one part of cement to two parts of fine aggregate (sand) and four parts of coarse aggregate (gravel). This may be produced by using 1 bag of cement (112 lb = $1\frac{1}{4}$ cu ft), $2\frac{1}{2}$ cu ft of sand and 5 cu ft of gravel. It should be noted, however, that for some types of work the 1:2:4 mix may not be satisfactory, and it may then be necessary to alter the ratio of fine to coarse aggregate.
A US gallon is equal to 0·83 Imperial gallon; a US bag of cement weighs 94 lb.

About the author

Professor Dr Gerd Däumel has been the Head of the Institute of Landscape Gardening and Landscape Architecture at the Hessian Teaching and Research Centre for Vine Culture, Fruit Growing and Horticulture at Geisenheim (Rheingau), Germany. As a landscape gardening consultant he has more particularly designed a large number of private and public gardens and estates. He has participated in regional planning and landscape architectural schemes in industrial regions. Also, he has engaged in extensive planning and consultant activities for municipalities and other local or regional authorities in Hesse, besides his numerous and varied teaching duties. Many of his articles dealing with problems of garden design and landscape architecture have appeared in professional journals, and he is the author of the books entitled *Über die Landesverschönerung* ('Beautifying the Countryside', 1961) and *Pflanzenbecken im Garten* ('Plant Pools in the Garden', 1961).